Classic
Sportives
South East England

About the Author

Colin Dennis has been riding bikes of one sort or another for longer than he dares to remember. His passion for road and off-road cycling has taken him all over the UK and continental Europe, both leading expeditions and for personal pleasure. Plotting, planning and escaping to new locations are pastimes that have driven him for many years, and working as both freelance copywriter and cycle guide provides a happy balance at home and work. Colin is never happier than when he's struggling up a steep climb behind a group, usually covered in mud, but as long as there's a warm tea shop involved – everything's possible. No legs were shaved in the making of this guidebook!

20
Classic Sportives
South East England

by Colin Dennis

2 POLICE SQUARE, MILNTHORPE, CUMBRIA LA7 7PY
www.cicerone.co.uk

First edition 2015

ISBN: 978 1 85284 743 2

Printed in China on behalf of
Latitude Press Ltd

A catalogue record for this
book is available from the
British Library.

All photographs
© Colin Dennis

This product includes
mapping data from the
Ordnance Survey® © Crown
copyright and database right
2015.

Mapping produced by Lovell
Johns Ltd

*This book is for Matthew –
A dolphin riding a bike*

Acknowledgements

I am very grateful to the friends and family
who have helped in getting this book out of
my head and onto paper. Special thanks go
out to Tony Gifford, Henry Bisset, Garry Du
Ploy and Lottie Dennis for the extra photos,
their wise input and fun company. I'm very
grateful to Paligap for the loan of the bike, and
to all at Mulebar for their energy and support.
Also, a huge debt of thanks must go out to all
the willing cyclists who were just out for a spin
but played such excellent models in many
photos; you were all heaven-sent. Finally
I'd like to thank my wife Sam for her tireless
support and patience, but especially for the
homemade chocolate cake supplied from the
broom-wagon.

Updates to this Guide

While every effort is made by our authors to
ensure the accuracy of guidebooks as they
go to print, changes can occur during the
lifetime of an edition. Any updates that we
know of for this guide will be on the Cicerone
website (www.cicerone.co.uk/743/updates),
so please check before planning your ride. We
also advise that you check information about
such things as transport, accommodation
and shops locally. Even rights of way can be
altered over time. We are always grateful for
information about any discrepancies between
a guidebook and the facts on the ground, sent
by email to info@cicerone.co.uk or by post
to Cicerone, 2 Police Square, Milnthorpe LA7
7PY, United Kingdom.

Front cover: All smiles on the summit of Box Hill (Route 12)

Contents

Map key 7
Overview map 8
Route summary table 10

INTRODUCTION   13

About sportives 14
The south east of England 14
Getting there and getting around 15
When to go 16
Accommodation 17
On the road 18
Safety 19
Emergencies 20
Equipment 21
Bike maintenance 22
The rules of the road 23
Maps 24
Navigation 24
Feed stations 25
Using this guide 26

Route 1 ▲ **Rattle and Hum**
                     Brockenhurst (New Forest) 29
Route 2 ▲ **Pony Express**
                     Brockenhurst (New Forest) 33
Route 3 ▲ **Kings of Meon**
                     Portsdown Hill (Hampshire) 37
Route 4 ▲ **Top and Tail**
                     Queen Elizabeth Country Park (South Downs) 43
Route 5 ▲ **Windoverstoke**
                     Andover (Hampshire) 47
Route 6 ▲ **The Gibbet**
                     Hungerford (Berkshire) 53
Route 7 ▲ **Dragon Slayer**
                     Hungerford (Berkshire and Wiltshire) 57

Route 8 ▲ **Isis**
Reading (Berkshire and Oxfordshire) 61

Route 9 ▲ **Devil's Highway**
Theale (Berkshire and Hampshire) 65

Route 10 ▲ **The Hog's Back**
Fleet (Hampshire and Surrey).............................. 69

Route 11 ▲ **Mud, Sweat and Gears**
Godalming (Surrey) 75

Route 12 ▲ **Surrey Hills**
Headley Heath (Surrey) 79

Route 13 ▲ **Reservoir Cogs**
Redhill (Surrey and Sussex)............................... 83

Route 14 ▲ **Park and Ride**
Withdean (East Sussex) 89

Route 15 ▲ **Weald-a-Beast**
Sevenoaks (Kent)... 95

Route 16 ▲ **Battle Plan**
Eastbourne (Sussex and Kent) 99

Route 17 ▲ **Merry Wives**
Marlow (Buckinghamshire and Berkshire)................... 103

Route 18 ▲ **The Wycombe Wanderer**
Marlow (Buckinghamshire and Oxfordshire)................. 107

Route 19 ▲ **Oxtail Loop**
Kidlington (Oxfordshire) 113

Route 20 ▲ **Ox and Bucks**
Kidlington (Oxfordshire and Buckinghamshire) 117

Appendix A Bike shops and cycle repair outfits........................ 121
Appendix B Useful contacts 124

▲ Grade 1   ▲ Grade 2   ▲ Grade 3   ▲ Grade 4

GPX FILES

for all routes can be downloaded for free at
www.cicerone.co.uk/member

Symbols on the route maps

~ route

~ shortcut

> route direction

▶ shortcut direction

🚲▷ start/finish point

🚲▷ alternative start/finish point

12🔗 route link

➊→ stage number

🔧 bike shop   ☕ café

🍺 pub

Features on the overview map

▨ Urban area

▨ National Park

▨ Area of Outstanding Natural Beauty

800m
600m
400m
200m
75m
0m

The route maps in this guide are reproduced at 1:250,000 (1cm = 2.5km)

| 0 | 2.5 | 5 km |
| 0 | 1 | 2 | 3 | miles |

ROUTE GRADES AND ABBREVIATIONS

Routes in this guide are graded as follows:

▲ perfect for cadence work with just the odd climb along the way

▲▲ a little lumpier but plenty of recovery miles

▲▲▲ quality hill-time with some sharp and testy climbs

▲▲▲▲ no retreat – no surrender

The following symbols are used in the route descriptions:

↑ straight ahead

← left

→ right

↰ left-hand

↱ right-hand

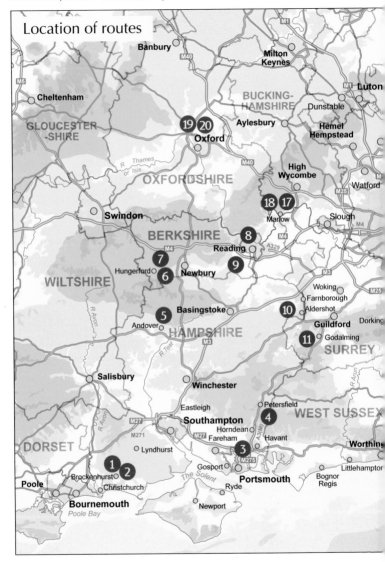

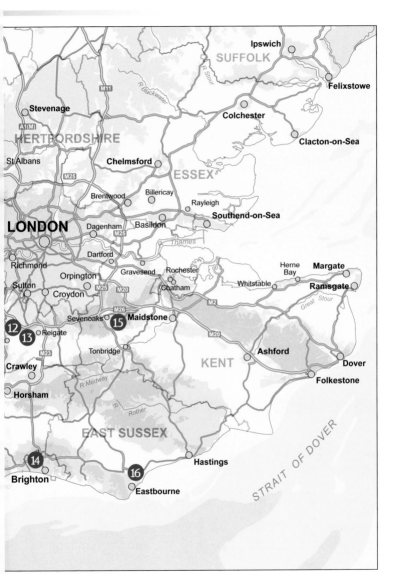

ROUTE SUMMARY TABLE

Route	Title	Location(s)	Start/Finish	Distance	Ascent	Grade	Time	Page
1	Rattle and Hum	New Forest	Brockenhurst central pay and display car park SU 298 024	80km (50 miles)	645m (2115ft)	▲	3–4hrs	29
2	Pony Express	New Forest	Brockenhurst central pay and display car park SU 298 024	85km (53 miles)	530m (1740ft)	▲	3–4hrs	33
3	Kings of Meon	Hants	Portsdown Hill car park SU 663 065	69km (43 miles)	890m (2920ft)	▲	3–4hrs	37
4	Top and Tail	South Downs	Car park at Queen Elizabeth Country Park SU 719 186	106km (66 miles)	1375m (4510ft)	▲	4hrs 30mins–6hrs	43
5	Windover-stoke	Hants	Andover Rugby Club car park SU 349 483	109km (68 miles)	780m (2560ft)	▲	4hrs 30mins–5hrs 30mins	47
6	The Gibbet	Berkshire	Hungerford long stay car park SU 336 686	75km (47 miles)	1090m (3575ft)	▲	3hrs–4hrs	53
7	Dragon Slayer	Berkshire and Wiltshire	Hungerford long stay car park SU 336 686	93km (58 miles); via short-cut: 62km (39 miles)	955m (3135ft); via short-cut: 655m (2150ft)	▲	4hrs–5hrs; via short-cut: 2hrs 30mins–3hrs 30mins	57
8	Isis	Berkshire and Oxon	Rivermead Leisure Centre car park, Reading SU 705 744	90km (56 miles)	895m (2935ft)	▲	4hrs–5hrs	61
9	Devil's Highway	Berkshire and Hants	Theale pay and display car park, near Reading SU 646 715	82km (51 miles)	425m (1395ft)	▲	3hrs–4hrs	65
10	The Hog's Back	Hants and Surrey	Hart Leisure Centre, Hitches Lane, Fleet SU 794 538	117km (73 miles)	885m (2905ft)	▲	5hrs–6hrs 30mins	69
11	Mud, Sweat and Gears	Surrey	South Street car park, Godalming SU 968 437	85km (53 miles)	1190m (3905ft)	▲	3hrs 30mins–5hrs	75

▲ Grade 1   ▲ Grade 2   ▲ Grade 3   ▲ Grade 4

Route	Title	Location(s)	Start/Finish	Distance	Ascent	Grade	Time	79
12	Surrey Hills	Surrey	Pay and display car park opposite Headley Heath Cricket Pitch, TQ 205 539; or Box Hill pay and display car park TQ 179 513	90km (56 miles)	1065m (3495ft)	▲	3hrs 30mins–5hrs	79
13	Reservoir Cogs	Surrey and Sussex	Gloucester Road car park, Redhill TQ 279 509	101km (63 miles)	1420m (4660ft)	▲	4hrs–6hrs	83
14	Park and Ride	East Sussex	Withdean Sports Complex car park TQ 297 076	100km (62 miles)	1410m (4625ft)	▲	4hrs–6hrs	89
15	Weald-a-Beast	Kent	Sevenoaks swimming centre long stay car park TQ 533 548; or Penshurst Station TQ 519 465	92km (57 miles)	1170m (3840ft)	▲	3hrs 30mins–5hrs	95
16	Battle Plan	Sussex and Kent	Sovereign Centre car park, Eastbourne TQ 632 006	90km (56 miles)	970m (3180ft)	▲	3hrs–4hrs 30mins	99
17	Merry Wives	Bucks and Berkshire	Oxford Road car park, Marlow SU 847 866	60km (37 miles)	540m (1770ft)	▲	2hrs 15mins–3hrs 30mins	103
18	The Wycombe Wanderer	Bucks and Oxon	Dean Street car park, Marlow SU 849 868	106km (66 miles); via short-cut: 72km (45 miles)	1410m (4625ft)	▲	4hrs 30mins–6hrs; via shortcut: 3hrs–4hrs	107
19	Oxtail Loop	Oxon	Kidlington Leisure Centre, Oxford SP 496 132	68km (42 miles)	430m (1410ft)	▲	2hrs 30mins–4hrs	113
20	Ox and Bucks	Oxon and Bucks	Kidlington Leisure Centre, Oxford SP 496 132	111km (69 miles)	615m (2020ft)	▲	4hrs–5hrs 30mins	117

Early morning training:
clear roads and a clear mind (Route 1)

Introduction

Sportive cycling is enjoying a boom-time. From chip-timed monumental feats of organisation and logistics to small club-run affairs, cycle sportives create a buzz all of their own. From social rider to wannabe racer, well-organised sportives cater for every standard of road cyclist. Pick any weekend from early spring through to late autumn and no matter where you live in the UK, you're bound to find a sportive event within reasonable distance from your door.

On the back of the UK's amazing cycling success in the Olympics, World Championships and the Tour de France, men and women have taken to road cycling in numbers not seen since the Victorian era. With the likes of Sir Chris Hoy, Sir Bradley Wiggins, Victoria Pendleton and Chris Froome filling the back pages of daily newspapers, UK cyclists are as recognisable today as football or motor racing stars.

Mortal riders take part in cycle sportives for many different reasons: fitness, challenge, obsession or raising money for charity. Whatever the reason, riders get out of bed at unearthly hours each weekend and ride in all weathers to become exhausted, yet exhilarated. This guide offers the perfect opportunity for riders of all abilities to challenge themselves over the most varied and scenic areas of the south east of England in preparation for their chosen sportive event.

Enjoy the ride!

The New Forest – open roads and slip streaming... heaven (Route 1)

About sportives

A sportive often includes a number of routes ranging from 25 miles up to 100 miles, or further. The varying route options enable riders of all abilities to challenge themselves against the clock without having to live by a strict training regime. Sportives are normally held on open roads and riders must obey the Highway Code. Each route will be well signposted by the organisers with strategically placed feed and drink stations peppered along the way. Most sportives now include chip-timing to accurately record the time of individual riders.

Arguably, the UK sportive scene has grown organically from a combination of the French 'randonnée cyclosportive' scene and British cycle club endurance rides. For many years cyclists have flocked, in their thousands, to participate in both open and closed road events over some of the toughest mountains in continental Europe. Some might say that modern British sportives are more akin to cycle club 'reliability trials'.

Popular during the winter months, reliability trials are long-distance club rides where riders and club racers concentrate on getting more 'relaxed or social' miles into their legs. Club runs seldom use route signage or feed stations, so riders are left to fend for themselves (hence, 'reliability'). Café stops are often an integral and important port of call during club runs.

Whatever the reasons, the ever-growing UK sportive season enjoys a

Sportives – raising money and smiles

calendar full of exciting and challenging rides in some of the most beautiful landscapes that these islands have to offer.

There are also a growing number of sportive events in the UK that are held on closed roads. Events such as the 'Etape Cymru' in North Wales and the 'Prudential London–Surrey 100' prove to be hugely popular, with riders entering in their thousands to complete these arduous rides in the safety of closed roads. But distance is not the only challenge facing sportive riders – hills play a major part in sportive rides, and conquering a severe climb is seen as one of the real tests of any given event. Sportives may not yet attract the mad-cap cycling supporters, or *tifosi*, as seen lining the mountain stages of the Tour de France, but a warm welcome is always on hand at the end of a sportive event.

Although sportive events are not races, many riders pride themselves in getting around in the quickest time possible and will look to improve on their times throughout the season. But one thing's for sure, sportive riders can enjoy a sense of achievement that few other amateur cyclists can. A hundred miles is a long way and should never be taken lightly. Train for the distance, train for the hills – enjoy the ride.

The south east of England

Within the broad regions of the UK: Hampshire, East and West Sussex, Kent, Berkshire, Surrey, Oxfordshire and Buckinghamshire all qualify as south east England. As far as training rides go, each county has enough beautiful countryside and variation of terrain to provide challenging routes, which prove ideal as testers of fitness in both body and mind.

As the most heavily populated area of the UK, life can be busy in England's south east, but this works in its favour too. An excellent system of trains, motorways and trunk roads make light work of delivering riders to wherever they want to cycle. Furthermore, the area offers sportive riders an eclectic mix of locations and country roads. From the brooding landscapes of the New Forest, to the rolling contours of the High Weald and Surrey Hills – mile upon mile of exciting terrain exists on which cyclists train and prepare for their favourite event. The number of cyclists riding every day in these beautiful areas proves that there's room for everyone.

Getting there and getting around

By car

All roads lead to London, and therefore the roads that shoot in and out of England's capital also reach out like a giant spider's web into the nooks and crannies of its south east. The M1 and M11 motorways allow easy access to the M25 circular from locations north, east and north east of the city, while the M40, M4 and M3 act likewise for car travellers approaching London from the Midlands and from locations to the city's west and south west.

The majority of routes within this guide are within easy access of motorways and main trunk roads and the start/finish points are quite often adjacent to a motorway or major road; such is the excellent road system of the region, you are never far from the beautiful landscapes that entertain classic sportive training rides.

By rail
Riders choosing to get to the area by rail should first check out National Rail enquiries (search 'Cycling and cyclists' on www.nationalrail.co.uk). Here you will find easy links to your nearest regional train provider and how you can book your bike onto a

train. Most trains to England's south east require you to travel through central London and then change station to get to your chosen sportive destination. Travelling by bike across London takes a little more planning; start by searching 'Bikes on public transport' at www.tfl.gov.uk, where Transport for London sets out the rules on taking non-folding bikes onto tubes, overground trains, river boats, buses and DLR.

Once you are in the area, the region is well-served by the rail network. All the main centres are served by mainline routes from London and other areas of south east England.

When to go
The south east of England boasts the warmest climate in the UK. It may

Slow down! North Gorley Tea Rooms beckon

Burning legs and lungs – get training! (Route 4)

not be exactly balmy, but, statistically, the area does enjoy the best of the weather. Realistically, however, it should be treated just the same as any other region in the UK: cold and wet in the winter, warm and damp with sunny bits in the summer, so dress accordingly – it's better to be warm than cold when out on your bike. Layer up and add some flexibility to your clothing.

Caution should be applied when ice and frost warnings are given in the winter months. Always ride with care in inclement weather as bad visibility can hide a cyclist from a vehicle driver quite easily. Use powerful front and rear lights in low light conditions. Wear something bright and reflective – do not be invisible to other road users.

Accommodation

From picture-postcard bed and breakfast cottages to five-star glitzy hotels and spas, south east England caters for all tastes. With many of the routes in this book based in Areas of Outstanding Natural Beauty (AONBs) or national parks such as the South Downs and New Forest, there is no shortage of self catering, bed and breakfast or hotel accommodation. See Appendix C for a list of websites that provide a good place to start your search for a good night's rest.

There are plenty of towns and areas to use as the perfect bases from which to explore the full potential of the region. To the west, Brockenhurst and Lyndhurst are ideal for the New Forest, Meon Valley and South Downs training routes, while Newbury and

Quiet Sunday mornings – priceless! (Route 20)

Hungerford provide easy access to Dragon Slayer, the Gibbet and Windoverstoke. Just south of London and the M25, the lively market towns of Godalming and Dorking are well situated to provide a springboard for The Hog's Back, Mud, Sweat and Gears, Surrey Hills and Reservoir Cogs, which all start centrally within the area covered by this guide. Further east, Brighton is close at hand for all the rides that pepper this corner of the region: Park and Ride, Weald-a-Beast and Battle Plan are within a short journey. To the north, Marlow and Oxford are excellent options to stay for routes such as Merry Wives, the Wycombe Wanderer, Oxtail Loop and Ox and Bucks.

On the road

Hills

Love them or hate them, hills are difficult to avoid if you ride sportives. Riding 50 to 100 miles can be a serious challenge in itself, but when you start adding long, grinding ascents and lung-busting climbs into the equation, the difficulty factor can multiply several times over.

Some routes in this book are unashamedly all about hill climbing. Every now and again it's worth including a shorter, harder climbing route such as the Gibbet, Kings of Meon or the second half of Surrey Hills as a specific training ride. It's also worth noting that a challenging climb at the

SAFETY

Cycle sportives and training rides are not races, and, unless it is held on closed roads, a sportive and the riders involved are bound by current traffic regulations and the Highway Code. Therefore it's worth getting into some good riding habits from the outset of your training regime. This will pay good dividends in your safety cycle-management come the day of the event.

Keep your bike in **good working order**, especially if you're getting in plenty of winter miles. Regular servicing of it is always a good thing; as is cleaning. Cleaning your bike is a good opportunity for close inspection, thereby avoiding potential problems later on. Check tyre pressures regularly too; correct tyre pressures are often the difference between an efficient and enjoyable ride and a puncture-fraught journey.

Be seen. Wear bright clothing and always fit a rear light. It's often as difficult to be seen on a bright sunny day as it is on a cloudy, overcast day. Always wear a cycle helmet.

Ride courteously, keep other road users in mind and give clear indications and signals of your intentions. Always check over your shoulder before you manoeuvre.

Be self-sufficient as much as possible. As a minimum of self-help and self-reliance, learn how to make small adjustments to your bike, repair punctures and fix a broken chain in the comfort of your home – don't leave it till it happens out on the road. If you do have a bike maintenance emergency on the road, see Appendix B for a list of bike shops.

Suggested minimum repair kit:

- pump
- CO_2 cartridges (x2) and inflator
- tyre levers (x3)
- spare tubes (x2)
- tube repair patches or puncture repair kit
- tyre repair patches
- multi-tool
- chain tool

Other essential items and considerations:

- fully charged mobile phone
- paper cash
- debit or credit card (taxi ride back to the start?)
- a riding partner or two
- let someone know where you are going and how long you're likely to be away

EMERGENCIES

Should a **serious injury** occur while out on a ride and you require hospital treatment, **dial 999 and request an ambulance**. You will need to give them your location and the state of your injuries. Always carry a fully charged mobile phone when out on a training ride.

If your injuries are less serious then consider calling 111 for the NHS urgent care facility. If you feel you are able to make it to an accident and emergency unit (A&E), see Appendix C for a list of local hospitals with full A&E facilities.

start of an event with fresh legs will feel like a very different beast after 50 miles or so. There are no shortcuts. If you want to avoid the walk of shame, train for the hills at every opportunity.

Yes, it would be naive to enter a ride such as the Fred Whitton Challenge in the Lake District and endure some of the most challenging climbs in England without suitable training. But there are plenty of challenging hills to be found in the south east of the country too, just don't get caught out by a lack of quality hill training. Plan ahead and make sure you know what you are getting into.

Read through this book, train on the routes that suit your aspirations and fitness, and as you progress through your training schedule choose a tougher course. Following the routes in this guidebook is also a great way to explore the varied and beautiful countryside of England's south east. Take your time, enjoy your riding and build up your distances and challenges before letting yourself loose on the world of cycle sportives.

Singletrack lanes

These are great for deterring lorries, but the myriad of narrow veins that criss-cross the British countryside will often be loose and gravely under your wheels. They will also be slippery with mud in the rain and, inevitably, the only car you'll meet will be skidding around that narrow corner. Singletrack lanes should be treated with respect. Keep your speed down on descents, ride in single file and expect the unexpected.

Cattle grids

They're everywhere in the New Forest, and they pop-up now and again on other routes too. They pose no problem as such, but it's always worth crossing them with a degree of caution when wet. Always cross them straight-on. Keeping a little momentum to free-wheel over cattle grids helps when approaching from uphill and standing up as you rattle across reduces weight on the back wheel to lessen pinch-flats.

Equipment

The bike

It may not be 'all about the bike', but a good-quality, lightweight road bike certainly makes life easier out on the road. A lightweight bike is generally easier to propel along the road than a heavier one, and is certainly less effort up the hills.

Make sure you ride a bike that is the right size for you; this is important if you want to get the maximum amount of power output from your bike and to avoid any injuries. A bike that is too small will be cramped and uncomfortable, whereas a bike that is too large will not allow enough stand-over height, which is potentially dangerous, and the handlebars will be too far away to reach for the brake levers.

Get along to your local bike shop to get specialist advice and to get sized up properly.

Helmet

Always wear a properly fitted cycle helmet. There are plenty of lightweight, good-quality helmets out there in the market to satisfy even the most reticent of helmet sceptics. You will more than likely have to wear a helmet to ride in a sportive anyway. Buy a good-quality helmet, look after it, and again get some advice and proper fitting from your local bike shop.

Cycle shorts

Never scrimp on buying cycle shorts: 100 miles is a long way to be sat down on a saddle and your rear will thank you for investing wisely. Bib shorts are

Suitable clothing always pays dividends (Route 8)

worth considering; they are extremely comfortable and don't cut into your waist at all. If you are riding often you should invest in at least a couple of pairs of shorts. Wash them regularly, and don't wear underwear underneath them.

Pedals and shoes
Clipless pedals and shoes are proven to be more efficient than traditional pedals without straps, and by quite some margin. If you do get into sportive cycling quite seriously and begin to include high mileage routes into your training programme then buying specialist clipless shoes such as Shimano Road SPDs makes complete sense.

Cycling apparel
Invest wisely in your cycling tops; buy the best that you can afford and only buy specific cycling jerseys made from either man-made fabrics, such as Polyester, or, in some cases, natural materials like Merino Wool, if retro styling is your bag. It's worth having a selection of short and long sleeve jerseys to allow for warm or cold weather. Again, pop into your local bike shop to get a taste of what's available.

When the weather turns cool it's worth considering layering up both upper body and legs. Cycling leggings will keep hardworking muscles warm, and a windproof and waterproof cycling jacket is a must. Buy the best that you can afford; there is some great kit out there that won't break the bank.

Gloves are a must-have item too; not only will they keep your hands warm but they soak up the sweat from your palms and help keep a safe grip on the handlebars. Wear short-fingered gloves when warm and full-fingered ones when cool. Waterproof cycling gloves should be considered in the winter or heavy rain conditions.

Cycle-specific glasses are highly recommended too: a fly in the eye at 20mph is not funny. Get clear lenses for rainy days, yellow lenses for low-light days and sunglasses for days when the sun decides to show its face. Three-in-one options are readily available so, unless you want to, it isn't necessary to buy three separate pairs.

Bike maintenance
Clean your bike regularly, preferably after each ride, but do so especially if the weather was inclement on your last ride. Grit and crud from the road will wear out your chain and components in no time if you don't wash them off. A quick hose-down and a little chain-specific oil will work wonders at prolonging the life of your bike.

Another reason for cleaning the bike regularly is that it is easy to spot any potential problems. When you get down into areas such as the spokes or bottom bracket, it's easier to inspect them as you clean your bike. Check bolts regularly for tightness too; don't over-tighten them but always check for safety.

It is worth having your bike serviced at least twice a year by a specialist bike shop. This may depend on how many miles you're putting in, but after a long winter or in the run-up to the sportive season, it's worth giving the bike some TLC so that it's ready for your event.

The rules of the road

Cyclists are responsible for their own behaviour on the road and are therefore bound by the Highway Code. Always ride responsibly and be courteous to other road users, especially horses and their riders. Always give clear indications as to your intentions before manoeuvring; the car driver behind you is not a mind reader, so indicate in plenty of time before turning.

Check over your right shoulder before manoeuvring or turning; this small but very important act could prevent anything nasty from happening – always check behind you before you turn or move out into traffic. Don't drift in and out of parked cars; stay out in the road until the obstacles end. Try not to ride too close to the edge either; there are drains and potholes waiting to eat you up. You will also be seen much earlier on a bend if you stay out from the edge. How you behave will reflect how other road users view other cyclists. Be an ambassador for your sport by riding responsibly – and remember to smile and wave (or at least nod) to other cyclists... please!

Expect the unexpected

Hills – what goes up...

Wishful thinking as far as cycling goes

MAPS

All the required OS Landranger Maps 1:50,000 for this guide can be found as follows:

- 164 Oxford
- 165 Aylesbury & Leighton Buzzard
- 174 Newbury & Wantage
- 175 Reading & Windsor
- 184 Salisbury & The Plain
- 185 Winchester & Basingstoke
- 186 Aldershot & Guildford
- 187 Dorking & Reigate
- 188 Maidstone & Royal Tunbridge Wells
- 195 Bournemouth & Purbeck
- 196 The Solent & Isle of Wight
- 197 Chichester & the South Downs
- 198 Brighton & Lewes
- 199 Eastbourne & Hastings

The New Forest offers timeless landscapes all the way

Some signs are obvious (Route 14)

Some signs are a little quirky (Route 13)

Navigation

The navigation in this guide is designed to be as intuitive and straightforward as possible. While none are onerous, some routes are easier to navigate than others. While clearly not in the game of stopping unnecessarily, there may be times when a quick reference to the route guide is required. If you've downloaded the route into your GPS, smartphone or other navigation aid, so much the better. Please remember: never read a map or guidebook while moving, always pull over first.

In lieu of direction arrows that would guide you around a sportive event, normal road signage now becomes your replacement arrows. The road signage throughout the routes is generally well maintained, but now and again there's always one that tries to trip you up with washed-out lettering; or on one or two occasions signs where letters aren't even there! It is important to spend a little time studying the routes beforehand and get a picture in your head of the day's ride.

Bear in mind that chatting away to your ride partner can cause wrong turns to be taken. Speed is another reason to miss a turn – going too fast downhill or pedalling hard with head down results in a loss of concentration and missing that all-important junction. Remember: these rides are training routes, not races. Stay in control of your bike, look where you're going, enjoy the beautiful scenery – and check the signage. Also, keep the book handy in one of your back pockets and download the relevant map into your GPS or smartphone.

Feed stations

A major factor to consider is energy and hydration replacement. On a long training ride, pubs, village shops, post offices, garages and cafés must act as feed and drink stations. Whether it's 25, 50 or 100 miles, it can feel like a long way on a bike when it's cold, wet and windy. Don't make it any harder for yourself; don't chance it on an empty tank.

To this end, make sure you carry plenty of food, water and energy bars, which can be crammed into rear pockets or stuffed into small feedbags on your bike. Eat and drink as you go along. Again, be self-reliant as much as possible; some pubs or

Don't fall off – fuel up

Toast and tea are all part of the regime (Route 9)

cafés may not be open if you're an early bird.

The old training maxim applies to everyone: drink before you're thirsty, and eat before you're hungry. Keep your energy levels up and replenish little and often as you go along – your performance and recovery levels will benefit dramatically.

Using this guide

The routes in this guide are designed to offer a happy medium across the distances involved and, importantly, provide some insight into what to expect when covering longer distances by bike.

Each route is designed for both newcomers and experienced sportive riders alike. Having built up a base level of fitness and stamina, any fledgling sportive riders will soon feel the

benefit of testing themselves against the distances and terrain involved. More experienced riders will enjoy the variation and challenge of discovering new routes as they test themselves in the most scenic areas across the south east of England.

As in any well-organised sportive route, the majority of mileage covered in this guide is on quiet country roads and lanes. B roads are kept to a minimum and are generally quiet as far as traffic is concerned. Major road sections are only used when unavoidable but integral to the route. Right-hand turns, especially on A and B roads, are kept to a minimum and used only where necessary. It would be almost impossible to only have left-hand turns; the route would be very short!

All the routes in this guide can be downloaded and are compatible for GPS. Each route is original in its concept, is the creation of the author and is designed to cover areas in which sportive rides are popular. Any similarity to existing sportive events is purely coincidental. The intention also is that the routes should be as close as possible to built-up areas. Not every route needs to be a 'destination' ride, but if you're lucky enough to live close to a route, riders can start from a more convenient point.

Route maps and profiles show you what to expect during each training ride and refreshment stops and bike shops have been plotted onto the maps with easy-to-spot icons. The route summary table in Appendix A gives an overview of the 20 routes detailing the basics: location, start and finish points, distance, ascent, grade and approximate time. Appendix B lists bike shops and cycle repair stations on a route-by-route basis, should you have any bike maintenance emergencies. Appendix C lists useful contacts such as accommodation and transport websites, sportive organisations and hospitals in the area.

Timings

Timings are often highly subjective when cycling and should only ever be used as a guide: café stops, puncture repairs, fitness levels, type of terrain (hilly rather than flat) and weather conditions are just a few internal and external influences on time taken to ride a particular route.

There will always be exceptions to the rule of course; if Sir Bradley Wiggins should decide that he wants to train on 'Reservoir Cogs' then he would be expected to be way inside the time frame.

Cadence

Performance cycling is all about optimising efficiency, and cadence is the cycling term for RPM or revolutions per minute. If cyclists turn their pedals at one rotation per second, they

And a bike wash to finish with – if the level's up (Route 2)

There's nowhere to hide when climbing (Route 13)

are deemed to be working at 60 RPM. Other factors do come into play, however: the selected gear, whether the terrain is rough or smooth and whether going up or down a hill, for example. Weather variations also play a part, especially wind conditions.

All these factors play their part in how cyclists ride. Ultimately, the desire is to pedal as smoothly and efficiently as possible to get the greatest return for the effort put in. It is better to spin the pedals efficiently rather than churn out a big gear and simply burn out the legs in no time.

Keep a higher cadence for more efficient pedalling, and aim for somewhere between 80 to 100 RPM. Don't worry too much about the speed at first, work on cycling efficiently; over a long distance a high cadence is the most effective way to ride.

Linking up routes

For riders who really want to test themselves before an event, a selection of routes in this guide join, or link together, at certain points along the way. Riders taking on the extra miles will experience what it's like to complete a full sportive event of approximately 100 miles or even more.

Route 1
Rattle and Hum (New Forest)

Start/Finish	Brockenhurst central pay and display car park SU 298 024
Distance	80km (50 miles)
Ascent	645m (2115ft)
Grade	
Time	3–4hrs
Feed stations	North Gorley Tea Rooms; Cider Press Café, Burley
Access	The main feeder roads to Brockenhurst are the A337, from the north, and the A35, from the south and west. From the A337 turn R just before the railway line onto Brookley Road. Continue into the town and turn R opposite Tesco Express into the car park at SU 298 024. From the A35 turn off at the Burley/Brockenhurst junction and follow signs to Brockenhurst. On reaching the ford turn R onto Brookley Road then turn L opposite Tesco Express to reach the car park.

For the sportive cyclist there's probably no finer location than the New Forest. Rattle over the cattle grids as you take in the brooding skylines and ancient tree-lined avenues, but, beware, a few surfaces here resemble nothing better than Paris–Roubaix Pave. Keep a watchful eye on the ponies too; they wander around like they own the place – which they do!

Overview

Heading out from Brockenhurst, the picturesque ornamental drive remains fairly narrow with plenty of potholes and rough edges; it doesn't get much better after the A35 as you climb up towards Bolderwood either. The road surfaces settle down after Bolderwood, Langford and Woodfalls, and although the roads get a bit rough and loose on some of the descents re-entering the forest at Hale, beyond Ringwood, the road into Bransgore is sublime, as are the final miles of slick tarmac to the finish.

1 Exit ➜ from the car park, cross the ford and then turn ➜ to follow Rhinefield Road to the A35. Go ⬆ at the **A35** onto Bolderwood Ornamental Drive, follow it up to a T-junction adjacent to Bolderwood car park and then turn ⬅ for Fritham. Continue under the **A31** to a road junction and turn ➜ towards **Stoney Cross**. At the end of the old

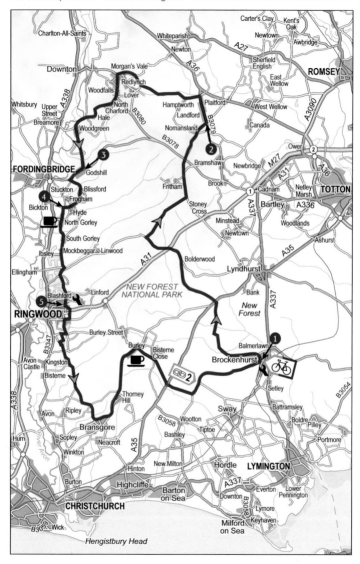

airfield road, turn ← towards **Fritham** and then carry on past the village to a road junction, keeping ← towards **Nomansland**. Go ↑ at the next crossroads and then turn ← to follow the **B3079** for **Landford**.

2 Continue for 2km before turning ← towards **Redlynch** and Downton (brown signpost for Country Club). On reaching the T-junction in **Woodfalls**, turn ← and go through the village. At a sharp bend beyond Woodfalls Inn, turn → through **North Charford** and **Hale** towards Woodgreen. The road gets wet and very narrow as it meanders into the Avon Valley. At the Horse and Groom Pub in **Woodgreen**, turn ← then ← again for Godshill.

3 At the T-junction in **Godshill** turn → to go past Sandy Balls Holiday Park and then take the next ← for **Blissford**. Turn → at the sign for the steep hill towards **Frogham** and **Hyde**, and at the junction at the top go ↑. At the bottom of the next descent take a sharp ← for North Gorley and Ringwood (easy to miss if travelling at speed).

4 Follow the Avon Valley floor past (or stop at) the **North Gorley Tea Rooms**, following the signs for Ringwood. At the ford crossing beyond Moyles Court School turn → for Rockford and stay in the valley floor until the outskirts of **Ringwood** are reached. At the roundabout beside The White Hart pub turn ← to continue over the **A31**. Turn → at the next roundabout and then ← onto Eastfield Lane (do not continue onto the A31).

5 Continue to the old Elm Tree Pub and turn → towards Burley and Bransgore. At the next T-junction, onto Moortown Lane, turn → for 700m then ← onto Long Lane, passing Ringwood Town FC. Follow this

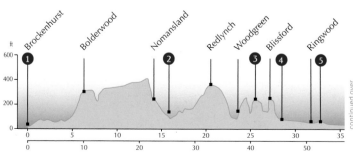

continued over

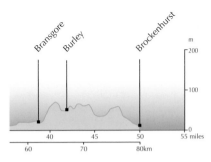

road in its entirety to the T-junction in **Bransgore**, and turn ← for Burley. At **Burley** village centre turn → to go uphill and past the golf course, continue under the **A35** and then carry on towards Brockenhurst.

Link to Route 2

To test your stamina and double your mileage, link this route to Pony Express by turning → for **Sway** before the final descent into Brockenhurst.

On returning to the ford in **Brockenhurst**, turn → for the town centre and car park.

Turning right in Burley for the run home

Route 2
Pony Express (New Forest)

Start/Finish	Brockenhurst central pay and display car park SU 298 024
Distance	85km (53 miles)
Ascent	530m (1740ft)
Grade	▲
Time	3–4hrs
Feed stations	Café, Lepe car park; The New Forest Inn, Emery Down
Access	The main feeder roads to Brockenhurst are the A337, from the north, and the A35, from the south and west. From the A337 turn R just before the railway line onto Brookley Road. Continue into the town and turn R opposite Tesco Express into the car park at SU 298 024. From the A35 turn off at the Burley/Brockenhurst junction and follow signs to Brockenhurst. On reaching the ford turn R onto Brookley Road then turn L opposite Tesco Express to reach the car park.

This route also goes through the New Forest but it has a slightly different feel to Rattle and Hum. The overall road quality is improved, being much less Paris–Roubaix and much more Paris–Nice; there's also an urban angle. It's as stunning a ride as Route 1, and there are many pleasant surprises to be found along the way. The inclusion of Hythe is designed not only to pull in riders from the Southampton and Portsmouth areas, but also to extend the route to loop out towards Exbury and Lepe. The eastern side of the forest is a little flatter too (not that the west side is exactly festooned with hills) but it's great for keeping your cadence up and working on your speed.

Overview

The road quality remains fairly good heading out of Brockenhurst and remains so until Pilley. The roads here are quiet until reaching Beaulieu, which can be unbelievably busy at peak weekends. Life goes quiet again towards Lepe, where your efforts are rewarded with a welcome pit-stop and dramatic views across the Solent. The navigation through Hythe is straightforward and intuitive, and the ride across the Forest beyond the A326 is simply stunning, as is the descent through the ornamental drive from Bolderwood back towards the finish.

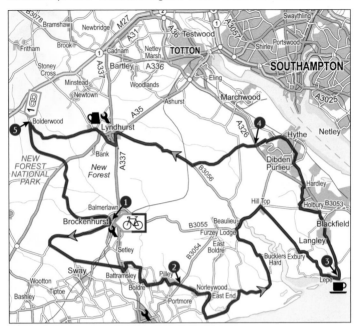

1 Exit ➜ from the car park, cross the ford and turn ⬅. Continue until you reach a road junction, signposted **Sway**. Turn ⬅ and follow the road to the B3055. Turn ⬅ onto this and then turn immediately ➜. On reaching the **A337** turn ➜ for 100m and then ⬅ onto Lower Sandy Down.

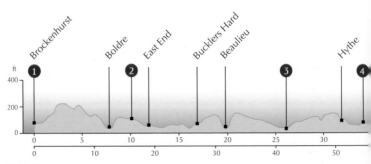

At Lepe you can almost touch the Isle of Wight from the café

Follow the narrow lane into the valley floor, keeping ➡ at the next junction, and climb up to the T-junction at **Boldre** opposite the Red Lion Inn. Turn ⬅, head up Pilley Hill and follow the road until it reaches the **B3054**.

2 Cross ⬆ and continue to **Norleywood**. At the T-junction in **East End**, turn ➡ onto Lymington Road and, after a short stretch, turn ⬅ onto Sowley Lane, signposted Bucklers Hard. Continue past the southern edge of Sowley Pond to a T-junction and turn ➡ onto St Leonards Road. Follow this to Salternshill Wood and turn ➡ for **Bucklers Hard**.

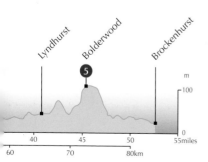

Continue along the lane to a T-junction with the B3055, and turn ➡ for Beaulieu. After 500m turn ➡ onto the B3054 to continue through **Beaulieu** and climb to a junction, signposted Exbury. Go ➡ and then ➡ again for Exbury Gardens and follow the lane to the seafront at **Lepe**.

3 Continue up Lepe Road, through **Blackfield**, to the crossroads with traffic lights. Turn ← onto Rollestone Road, signposted Beaulieu. As the road starts to descend (after 1km) turn → into the woods of Park Lane, continuing to a T-junction. Turn ← onto Lime Kiln Lane to reach a roundabout on the **A326**, and take the second exit for **Hythe**. Continue to a major T-junction and turn →, then keep ← along Southampton Road. After 1.5km, turn ← onto Claypits Lane to head towards a leisure centre. At a small roundabout turn → for Sizer Way, then turn ← at the next roundabout and continue to another roundabout on the A326.

There's no signpost! Turn right onto Park Lane for Hythe

4 Go ↑ for Beaulieu Road Station, ↑ at the next junction and continue on to reach a junction with the **B3056**. Turn →, go past the station and follow the road to **Lyndhurst**. At a T-junction turn ← and follow the **A35**, signposted Christchurch, around the southern edge of Lyndhurst. After leaving the village, turn → into Emery Down and turn ← at New Forest Inn to reach **Bolderwood**.

Link to Route 1
Going for an epic? Test your stamina to the max and double your mileage by linking to Rattle and Hum at **Bolderwood**.

5 Just beyond Bolderwood car park turn ← and descend to the A35. Go ↑ onto Rhinefield Ornamental Drive to **Brockenhurst**, turn ← across the ford to the High Street and ← into the car park.

Route 3
Kings of Meon (Hampshire)

Start/Finish	Portsdown Hill car park SU 663 065
Distance	69km (43 miles)
Ascent	890m (2920ft)
Grade	▲▲
Time	3–4hrs
Feed stations	Van at the start, open 24/7, 364 days a year; Café, West Meon, behind the post office (closed on Sundays); The Thomas Lord, West Meon; Lotts Tea Rooms, below Cams Hill
Access	To reach Portsdown Hill from Portsmouth, cross the M27 via the Northern Road to the A3. Near the summit of the long climb turn L onto the slip road, signposted Southwick. At the next junction turn L for the car park at SU 663 065, which will be on your left.

The backdrop of Portsmouth and its historical dockyard acts as a dramatic start and finish line to Kings of Meon. The area of the Meon Valley, north of Portsmouth, is notable for its soft blend of rolling countryside, ancient fortifications and its fast-flowing river. But, more importantly, it's probably as good as it gets as far as hill-based training rides go. As the name suggests, Kings of Meon is as much about bagging the hills and the chance to gain some fantasy Polka Dot Jersey points as it is about experiencing the pure joys of a challenging sportive training ride.

Overview

After descending from Portsdown Hill you begin to wonder exactly where the hills are, but don't worry, they come right out of nowhere as you approach Clanfield and remain a constant companion until the very last turn of the cranks. Traffic is light, the navigation straightforward and stunning views punctuate every hilltop. Remember – from the top of every great climb, there's always a great descent.

1 Turn ← out of the car park and, after 100m, turn → onto Widley Walk, next to the pub. Continue down to the T-junction and turn → and, at the next junction, turn ← for **Denmead**. Turn → after Furzeley Golf Course and → again onto the B2150. After 400m turn ← onto Soake

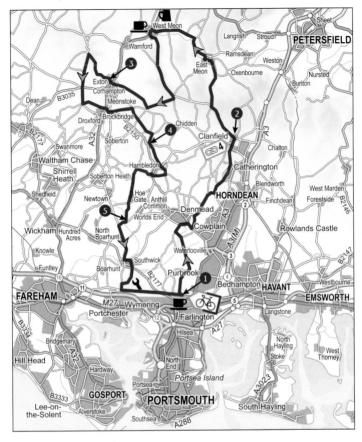

Road and continue to a T-junction. Turn ➜ and then continue along Day Lane to reach another T-junction, and turn ← for Clanfield. At the Rising Sun Inn in **Clanfield**, turn ← for East Meon.

Link to Route 4
If Kings of Meon isn't tough enough for you, link this route to Route 4 by turning ➜ at Clanfield then ➜ again over the A3 to pick up Top and Tail in **Chalton**.

Where the climbing starts – the Rising Sun Inn, Clanfield

Climbing out of Exton – The White Way round

2 Follow the lane, climbing and then descending into **East Meon**. Go through the village, turning ← in front of the church, and continue to **West Meon**. Turn ← onto the **A32** for 250m, then turn ← onto Station Road and climb to a T-junction. Turn ← for Old Winchester Hill and continue past the nature reserve to a three-way junction at Teglease Down. Turn → and follow the road around to the →. Nearing the end of the long straight descent, turn → onto Stocks Lane, signposted Corhampton. At the bottom of the lane turn → through the dismantled railway bridge, then turn ← to cross straight over the A32.

3 In **Exton** turn ←, following signposts for the South Downs Way, and follow the lane around to the → to climb The White Way. At the top of the climb turn ←, signposted Exton (HGV), then cross over the **B3035**. At a crossroads, turn ← down Sheep Pond Lane. Cross over the A32 onto the **B2150**, continuing under the railway arch, and then turn ← onto Watton Lane (not signposted) to the crossroads at the top of the climb. Turn → here, then continue ↑ at the next crossroads to reach a small T-junction. Turn ←, following a descent for 600m, then turn sharp →. At the next crossroads go ↑.

4 After 100m turn L onto Church Lane and follow this to the road junction in **Hambledon**, at which turn ← then immediately → up Pelham Hill. At the top of the climb turn → at the Rushmere signpost (easy to miss) and descend to a T-junction with the **B2150**. Turn → here then

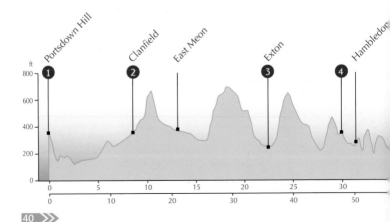

The amazing finishing stretch above Portsmouth

turn ← in front of Lotts Tea Rooms and continue to a crossroads at Hoe Cross Farm. Turn ←, signposted Southwick. At the next T-junction turn ← then immediately →, and continue to another T-junction.

5 Turn → towards Shoot Hill and take the next ← onto a narrow lane for **Southwick**. Continue through the village then turn → at a junction to reach the roundabout on the **B2177**. Go ↑ and climb Crooked Walk Lane to come to the crossroads atop Portsdown. Turn ← to head past Fort Southwick and reach a roundabout. Take the second exit and continue past Fort Widley to return to the car park.

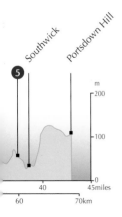

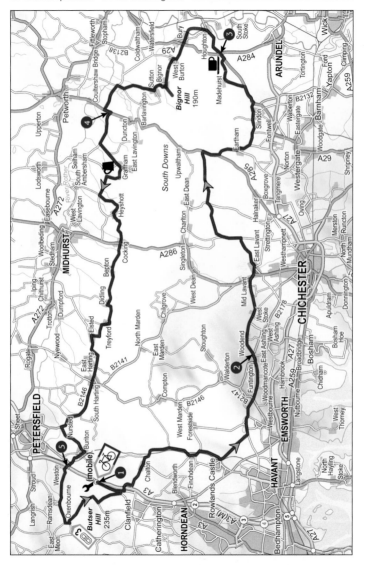

Route 4
Top and Tail (South Downs)

Start/Finish	Car park at Queen Elizabeth Country Park SU 719 186
Distance	106km (66 miles)
Ascent	1375m (4510ft)
Grade	
Time	4hrs 30mins–6hrs
Feed stations	Café at the start/finish; café in the car park at Whiteways roundabout adjacent to the A29; The White Horse Inn, Graffham
Access	The only vehicle entrance to Queen Elizabeth Country Park is via the A3 just south of Petersfield. Exit the slip road, signposted Queen Elizabeth Country Park, and follow the directions into the car park at SU 719 186.

Top and Tail is one big loop of the western edge of the South Downs National Park where the scenery is superb at every turn of the pedal. The ride is dominated by two tough climbs: the 'sting in the tail' that is Bignor Hill at the eastern edge is included as an option only, but the 'top-out' near the summit of Butser Hill at the western extremity is an integral part of the route that kicks in right at the end. 'Top and Tail' feels like a long way from home, with cafés and bike shops in short supply, but apart from that, it's a cracking ride, especially if you include mighty Bignor Hill.

Overview

A noisy start, along the cycle path beside the oncoming traffic of the A34, is followed by the quiet back roads of the South Downs National Park. Keep the high ridgeline on your left shoulder as you head east; with the short climb to Goodwood Race Course behind you, the views and miles are easily eaten up. After Bignor, the return journey offers you a mirror image as you head back west. Keep the high ground on your left again as you pick off village after village that punctuate the road home.

1 Turn → out of the car park, signposted Petersfield, go under the **A3** and turn ← up onto the cycle path. Turn ← again, and follow the cycle path alongside the oncoming A3. Keep → on reaching the narrow lane and

Glorious Goodwood – where the going's always good

continue to the roundabout, where you turn ← for Chalton. Turn ← in **Chalton**, continue over the railway line and follow the signposts for Rowlands Castle. Turn ← at **Rowlands Castle** onto Woodberry Lane, just before the railway arches beside the Castle Inn. Continue to the T-junction and turn ← to continue to Funtington.

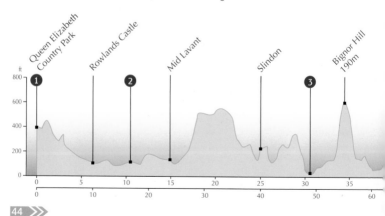

2 On exiting **Funtington** on the B2149, turn ← onto a narrow lane (not signposted) for **West Stoke** and keep ← at the next junction for Mid Lavant. In **Mid Lavant**, turn → onto the **A286** and then turn ← onto Sheepwash Lane. Keep ← at **East Lavant** and continue to the T-junction, turning ← up towards Goodwood Race Course. Turn → just before the grandstand and continue through woodland to reach the **A285**. Turn → for 1km, then turn ← for Slindon. On exiting **Slindon** turn ← onto Mill Lane and continue to the junction with the **A29**. After 1km leave the A29 briefly, turning ← for **Madehurst**. Turn ← to return to the A29, and then at the roundabout take the second exit onto the B2139.

3 Descend into **Houghton** and turn ← in the village for Bury, then ← at the junction in **Bury** and carry on to the A29. Go → onto the A29 then ←, signposted West Burton and Bignor. Follow signs to Bignor, turn ← at a blue signpost (unsuitable for HGV) and ← again past a farm to climb **Bignor Hill** to the small car park. Retrace your tracks to **Bignor**, turn ← for Sutton and follow the road signposted for Petworth. Continue to the crossroads and turn ← past the northern end of Burton Mill Pond to reach the **A285**. Turn ← onto the narrow path for 400m, then turn → across the A285 for Graffham.

4 Continue to a crossroads and turn ← for Graffham. After the Foresters Pub in **Graffham** turn → to another crossroads, then ← for Hoyle and Heyshott. At the church in **Heyshott** take the sharp ← onto the farm road and continue to the A286 in **Cocking**. Turn ← onto the **A286**,

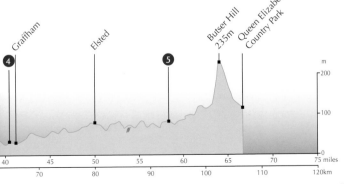

You can almost taste the finish from South Harting – just one thing in the way: Butser Hill

then turn ➡ for Bepton, Didling and Treyford. On leaving **Treyford**, turn ⬅ for Elsted. At the T-junction in **Elsted** turn ⬅ for South Harting. Turn ➡ onto the **B2146**. After 4km turn ⬅ for a sharp climb opposite Stanbridge Farm and continue to **Buriton** roundabout.

5 Go ⬆ at the roundabout, carry on under the **A3** and turn ➡, following signs for East Meon. Continue to follow signs for East Meon until reaching **Oxenbourne**.

Link to Route 3
For an epic that's definitely worth a medal, link this ride to Kings of Meon by turning ➡ at **Oxenbourne** to reach **East Meon**.

6 At Oxenbourne, go ⬅ beside a small stream in front of a row of cottages up Harvesting Lane. On the shoulder of **Butser Hill**, turn ➡ then ⬅ down Hogs Lodge Lane. Go ⬅ at the bottom of the descent, then ⬅ again to follow the cycle path alongside the A3. Turn ➡ under the A3 to return to Queen Elizabeth Country Park.

Route 5
Windoverstoke (Hampshire)

Start/Finish	Andover Rugby Club car park SU 349 483
Distance	109km (68 miles)
Ascent	780m (2560ft)
Grade	
Time	4hrs 30mins–5hrs 30mins
Feed stations	The Vine At Hannington
Access	From the north, turn off the A303 onto the A343, and follow it onto Churchill Way to a large roundabout. Turn L to a smaller roundabout and turn L onto Goch Way. Continue to a mini roundabout and turn R, then on to another roundabout, taking the fourth exit into the rugby club car park at SU 349 483.

This stunning ride, notwithstanding the initial gentle climb, is one of the flattest and easiest routes to navigate, but don't let this fool you; it's a long ride and should be taken seriously. The route overall is flatteringly fast and combines some of the finest rolling countryside that Hampshire has to offer; and with summer fields filled with poppies you could easily be cycling through Flanders at times. Windoverstoke is the perfect route for getting that all-important speed and cadence training just right.

Overview

After gently climbing north, the delights of the Bourne Valley are soon reached for a superb flowing section. After a rest-stop at The Vine At Hannington, the route is blessed with another series of fine descents through North Oakley, Ashe Warren and into Sutton Scotney. From here, the terrain continues to gently undulate without the long straights of the northern half of the ride. Following the beautiful Test Valley back towards Andover is, thankfully, very kind to tired legs.

 Exit the car park and take the third exit off the roundabout onto Hungerford Lane. At the top of Hungerford Lane keep → and descend Conholt Hill to a T-junction. Turn → and continue to the **A343** at **Hurstbourne Tarrant**. Turn → then immediately ← onto the B3048 (Stoke Road) through **St Mary Bourne** to the railway viaduct and turn ← at the crossroads onto Harroway (signposted Whitchurch and A34).

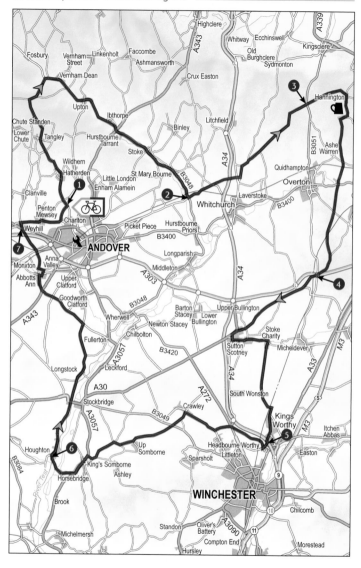

Swift riding through the Bourne Valley

2 Follow the Harroway back under the railway line to a double junction and take the second ← onto a singletrack road (signposted A34 avoiding low bridge). Cross over the **A34**, then go ↑ at the next crossroads to a T-junction. Turn ← and continue until the road becomes the B3051, and turn →, signposted Overton.

3 Take the next ← up Meadham Lane and continue to a small triangular junction in **Hannington** and turn → past The Vine to continue south through North Oakley and **Ashe Warren** to the B3400. Go across the **B3400** onto Burley Lane, and over the railway line at South Litchfield to reach a T-junction just north of the A303.

4 Turn → at the T-junction, then ← under the **A303**. Go immediately → onto the west-bound slip road and take the next ←, signposted Micheldever Station and Sutton Scotney (do not go onto the A303!). Continue to the **A30** at **Sutton Scotney** and turn ←, then take the next ← onto Oxford Road. At the memorial, turn ← for Wonston and Stoke

Rose-tinted riding near Ashe Warren

Charity. At **Stoke Charity** turn ➜ onto Old Stoke Road, go over the railway line and descend slowly before turning ➜ into Springvale Road just before the King Charles Pub in **Kings Worthy**.

5 Carry on under the **A34**, turn ➜ just past the garden centre onto Down Farm Lane and continue to a roundabout. Take the second exit onto

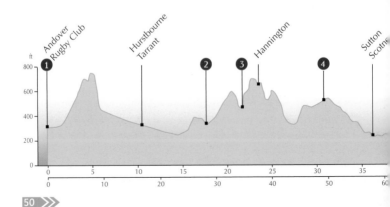

Turning left at the village pond in Crawley

Stud Lane. At the next T-junction turn → for **Crawley**, then turn ←
opposite the village pond. Go ↑ at the crossroads with the **B3049** to
reach **King's Somborne**. Here turn ← onto the **A3057** for 700m and
then turn → for **Horsebridge**. Keep → at the small triangle junction to
go past the John of Gaunt Pub and over the **River Test**, and turn → for
Stockbridge.

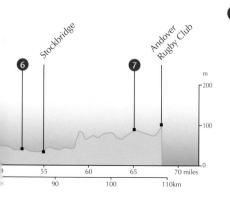

6 Follow the Test
Valley to the A30 in
Stockbridge and go ↑
onto Longstock Road.
Follow this road to a
crossroads and turn
← onto Fullerton Road
towards Red-Rice (not
signposted). Continue
to the **A343** and go
↑ into **Abbotts Ann**
to the T-junction with
Cattle Lane. Turn →

Roadside 'tifosi' in Upton

then ← onto Red Post Lane. At the four-way junction over the railway line dog-leg → then ← to stay on Red Post Lane and continue over the A303 to the T-junction with the A342 in Weyhill.

7 Turn ← onto the A342 then immediately turn → into Rectory Lane. Continue to a crossroads and turn → along Foxcotte Lane towards **Charlton**. At the first roundabout turn ← to continue along Foxcotte Lane. At the next roundabout take the third exit back into Andover Rugby Club.

Route 6
The Gibbet (Berkshire)

Start/Finish	Hungerford long stay car park SU 336 686
Distance	75km (47 miles)
Ascent	1090m (3575ft)
Grade	
Time	3–4hrs
Feed stations	Cafés on Hungerford High Street; George Inn, Vernham Dean
Access	Hungerford is easily accessible from Newbury via the A4. Leave the A4 at Eddington and follow signs into Hungerford town centre. Turn R at the mini roundabout beside the large clock; the car park at SU 336 686 is just on the right.

A 'gibbet' is a gallows-type structure from which, in days gone by, dead or dying bodies of criminals were hung on public display, to deter other people from committing criminal acts. But for clean-living cyclists, this modern-day gibbet is all about hill climbing and, with no fewer than six climbs of note crammed into the route, you'll find plenty of quality training to be had. However, with long sweeping descents punctuating the climbs, the rewards for your efforts are spectacular. The views and overall quality of the Gibbet make it all worthwhile and any pain is soon forgotten – honest!

Overview
The climb up Inkpen Hill to the Gibbet is a real taster for what's coming your way. The two subsequent climbs up to the brilliantly named village of Faccombe will keep you thinking. Conholt Hill is a local favourite challenge and the climb out of Shalbourne up the Rivar Road will test tired legs too. With plenty of other minor climbs along the way, muscles will be tight and blood will pump; this one's all about the climbs.

1 Turn ← out of the car park to the roundabout. Turn → then immediately ← along Park Street and continue through the Common to the junction with the High Street in **Kintbury** and turn ←. Turn → opposite the post office onto Inkpen Road and continue along Blandys Hill and Rooksnest Lane, across **Inkpen Common** to **Upper Green**. Turn ← onto Bell Lane. Continue to the T-junction and turn ← up Inkpen Hill towards the 'Gibbet' up on the skyline ahead.

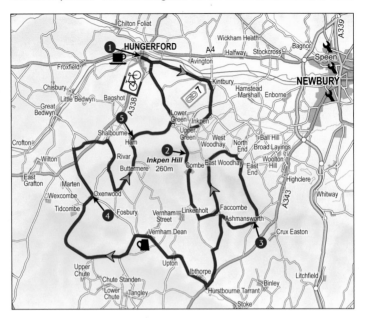

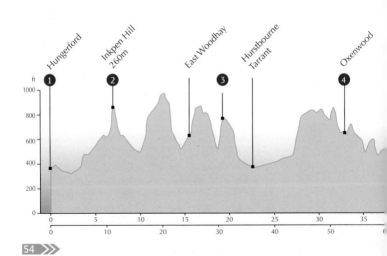

2 At the top of **Inkpen Hill** carry straight on and descend south through **Combe**, keep ← for Netherton and turn ← for Faccombe. Keep ← as you reach **Faccombe** and turn ← at the T-junction. Follow the lane north until reaching the junction high above the escarpment and turn → down towards East Woodhay. Keep → in **East Woodhay** and climb up to the T-junction in **Ashmansworth**. Turn → into the village, then → again at the memorial green to return to Faccombe.

3 After climbing up to the edge of Faccombe take the first ← to descend to a T-junction, and turn ← again to join the **A343**. Turn → into **Hurstbourne Tarrant** and → again for Ibthorpe and Vernham Dean. Just beyond **Vernham Dean**, turn ← up Conholt Hill towards Conholt Park and Tangley to a road junction at the top of the climb and turn → onto Chute Causeway towards Chute and Oxenwood. Keep → at the next junction to descend to a T-junction and turn → into **Oxenwood**.

4 On reaching the village turn sharp ← and continue to the **A338**. Go ↑ across the main road to a crossroads and turn → for Shalbourne. Turn → at the next junction and cross the A338 again to reach **Shalbourne**. On reaching the Plough Inn turn → onto Rivar Road and, as you reach the top of the climb, turn ← towards Fosbury. On reaching the junction

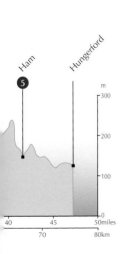

What the Romans did for cycling – Chute Causeway

Turn right for home at the Crown and Anchor in Ham

beside the airstrip turn ← onto Ashley Drove Road towards Buttermere and Henley.

5 Descend into **Ham** and turn → onto Spray Road beside the Crown and Anchor towards Inkpen. On reaching **Lower Green** turn ← onto Craven Road. Turn ← at the Y-junction and follow Inkpen Road north back to Hungerford Common. Turn ← onto the High Street in **Hungerford** and turn → then immediately ← to return to the car park.

Link to Route 7

Need more hills? Churn up your insides on the Gibbet, head back to **Kintbury**, and slay the dragon to recuperate.

Route 7
Dragon Slayer (Berkshire and Wiltshire)

Start/Finish	Hungerford long stay car park SU 336 686
Distance	93km (58 miles); via shortcut: 62km (39 miles)
Ascent	955m (3135ft); via shortcut: 655m (2150ft)
Grade	
Time	4–5hrs; via shortcut: 2hrs 30mins–3hrs 30mins
Feed stations	Hungerford High Street; Café in Lambourn; White Horse, Woolstone; deli/café in Aldbourne
Access	Hungerford is easily accessible from Newbury via the A4. Leave the A4 at Eddington and follow signs into Hungerford town centre. Turn R at the mini roundabout beside the large clock; the car park at SU 336 686 is just on the right.

Ideal for both princes and princesses, Dragon Hill is straight out of an Arthurian legend. This cracking climb holds commanding views right across the Vale of the White Horse and it's easy to imagine Avalon on high as you steel your way to the top.

Overview

With a lovely opening run along the Kennet Canal and up the Lambourn Valley, gentle is the word right up until you challenge the dragon. After slaying the beast, there's time to polish your armour as you hit the flat ground of the Vale, but this is where the tempo changes once again as you head south. Through the remaining countryside, the hills come at you in steady formation almost to the end of the ride.

Fox Hill – a sly little climb

1 Turn ← out of the car park to the roundabout. Turn → then immediately ← along Park Street and continue through Hungerford Common to the junction with the High Street in **Kintbury**. Turn ← and continue to the junction with Newbury Road, then turn →, signposted for Hamstead Marshall. On leaving **Kintbury** turn ← onto Irish Hill Road, signposted Marsh Benham, and continue to the railway crossing just beyond the **Kennet Canal**.

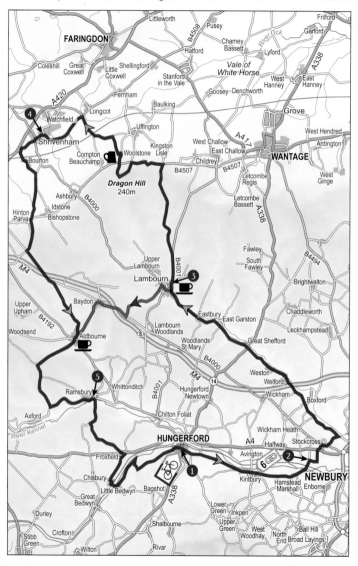

Warming up towards Lambourn

2 Take the next ➡ and continue to the **A4** at Gravel Hill. Go ⬆ onto Church Road and, on reaching the **B4000**, turn ➡ and then take the next ⬅ onto Chapel Road, signposted Woodspeen. Turn ➡ to descend Snake Lane and at the T-junction at the bottom turn ⬅ to follow the Lambourn Valley floor, continuing under the **M4** and through **Welford** to the **A338**. Turn ➡ then ⬅ and continue to Lambourn village.

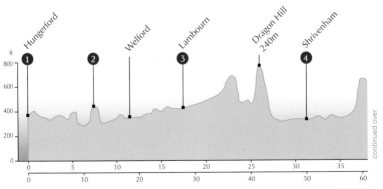

continued over

Shortcut to Aldbourne

If your charger is having a bad day, cut this route short at **Lambourn**. Continue onto the **B4000**, turn ← onto Baydon Road, turn → at the T-junction and then turn ← in **Baydon** to pick up the route again in **Aldbourne**.

3 Turn → onto the **B4001** in **Lambourn** and continue for 2km, turning ← at the signpost for Seven Barrows. Continue to the **B4507** and turn ←. Continue to the junction, signposted Uffington White Horse, and turn ← to climb **Dragon Hill**. At the end of the road turn → and descend back to the B4507 and go ↑ into **Woolstone**. Turn ← for Shrivenham and continue to a T-junction. Turn ←, continue under the railway bridge to a crossroads and turn ← for Shrivenham.

4 At the roundabout in **Shrivenham** turn ← onto the High Street and continue ↑ at the next roundabout. Stay on this road to the junction just before the **A420**, where you turn ← for Bourton. Continue through **Bourton** to a junction, and turn → then next ← for Fox Hill. At the cross-roads at the top turn ← and go under the **M4**. Turn → for **Aldbourne** and then go → to the **B4192**. Turn → then ← past the post office and deli onto Marlborough Road, continue to the T-junction and then turn ← for Ramsbury.

5 Turn → by The Bell, in the centre of **Ramsbury**, then → again over the **River Kennet**, signposted Froxfield, and a 17 per cent hill climb. At the junction with the **A4** turn → then immediately ← up Brewhouse Hill for **Little Bedwyn**. At the small crossroads above the village turn ←, turn ← again to cross the **Kennet Canal**, and turn ← again to fol-

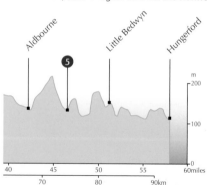

low the canal bank. Continue to a small junction and turn →, signposted North Standen (do not continue left over the canal towards the A4), and continue into **Hungerford** to return to the car park on the ←.

Link to Route 6

Got a thirst for challenging contours? Return to **Kintbury** and take on The Gibbet.

Route 8
Isis (Berkshire and Oxfordshire)

Start/Finish	Rivermead Leisure Centre car park, Reading SU 705 744
Distance	90km (56 miles)
Ascent	895m (2935ft)
Grade	
Time	4–5hrs
Feed stations	Jan Marie Café, Goring
Access	From the M4 take the A33 towards the city centre and pick up the A329. Once over the railway lines, turn L at the roundabout onto Caversham Road. Continue to the next roundabout and turn L onto Richfield Avenue, signposted Rivermead Leisure Complex. At the next mini roundabout turn R into the car park at SU 705 744.

Architecturally, Reading may not win any awards for romanticism, but this busy location lends itself perfectly as a starting point to explore the Thames Valley area. In no time you're out in the middle of perfect cycling terrain; with gentle climbs, smooth roads and light traffic, Isis is a route to savour. At Goring, where the ride crosses the ancient Ridgeway route, there are some stunning views west towards Didcot.

Overview

Climbing swiftly out of Reading, you're soon in gentle, rolling countryside and passing some interesting antennas near Devil's Hill. The road surfaces and lack of contours enable good cadence to be maintained all the way to Goring and Streatley. Here Streatley Hill makes a bold statement but, with excellent stretches of easy riding, the pain is soon forgotten. After a little more legwork beyond Pangbourne, the run into Reading is a great way to finish off.

1 Exit the car park and turn ← onto Richfield Avenue. Turn ← at the roundabout, go over the **River Thames** and then turn → at the lights onto Church Street. Turn ← at the traffic lights beside the Prince of Wales pub onto the B481 (Peppard Road) and continue to Emmer Green. At the top of **Emmer Green**, turn → onto Kiln Road to continue to a small three-way junction at Mays Green and turn ←, signposted

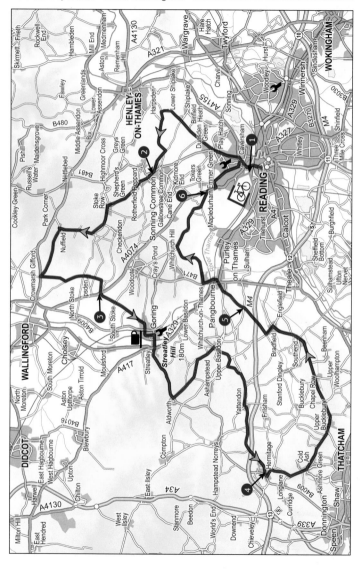

Crossing the Thames at Goring

Harpsden Bottom. Descend to a T-junction, turn ← and climb Devil's Hill to another T-junction.

2 Turn → and continue to a T-junction in **Sonning Common**. Turn → then immediately ← onto Stoke Row Road. Continue to the T-junction in **Stoke Row** and turn ← for Nuffield. In **Nuffield** turn ← onto Nuffield Hill and continue to a small crossroads just before the A4130. Turn ← and continue to a T-junction. Turn ← and descend through **Ipsden** to a junction at Braziers College and turn →. Continue to the **A4074** and go ↑.

3 Follow the road to the B4009 in **Goring**, go ↑ under the bridge and keep ← along Cleeve Road. At Glebe Road turn → and continue to the High

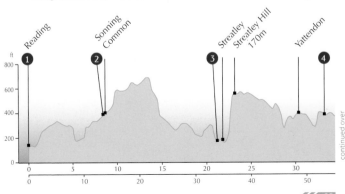

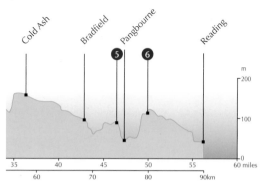

Street. Turn → to go over the **River Thames** at **Streatley** and go ↑ at the lights to climb **Streatley Hill**. Follow the B4009 to Aldworth. In **Aldworth**, turn ← onto Reading Road and continue to Upper Basildon. At a small crossroads just before **Upper Basildon** turn →, signposted Ashhampstead, and continue to a T-junction. Turn ← then → onto Yattendon Lane, go through **Yattendon** and continue over the M4 into **Hermitage**.

4 Turn ← onto the **B4009** and then turn sharp ← onto Marlston Road, signposted Marlston and with a blue warning sign for a low bridge. Go under this bridge, turn → onto Slanting Hill and continue to a T-junction. Turn ← for **Cold Ash** and turn ← at a crossroads onto The Ridge. Continue through Turners Green to **Chapel Row** followed by **Southend** and turn ← at Southend's war memorial for Bradfield. Turn ← in the centre of **Bradfield** onto St Andrews Close, then turn → onto Dark Lane. Go under the **M4** to a crossroads.

5 Go ↑ and descend to a T-junction in **Pangbourne**. Turn → to the A340, turn ← to a mini roundabout, then go → and immediately ← onto the **B471**, signposted Whitchurch. Go under a narrow railway bridge and cross over the River Thames into **Whitchurch**. As the road steepens, turn → at the post box onto Hardwick Road and continue around and up the steep climb to the crossroads at Goring Heath. Turn →, continue to the **A4074** and turn →.

6 After a short stretch on the A4074, turn ← onto Shepherds Lane and continue between houses along Kidmore Road to a mini roundabout. Turn ← then → onto Hemdean Road to a T-junction with Church Street. Turn → to cross the River Thames, turn → at a roundabout and follow Richfield Avenue back to the car park.

Route 9
Devil's Highway (Berkshire and Hampshire)

Start/Finish	Theale pay and display car park, near Reading SU 646 715
Distance	82km (51 miles)
Ascent	425m (1395ft)
Grade	▲
Time	3–4hrs
Feed stations	Shops and cafés on the High Street, Theale; The Leather Bottle, Mattingley; The Bakery, Bramley (closes at 1pm on Sundays)
Access	Exit the M4 at junction 12 and follow signs for Theale. On reaching the high street in Theale, turn R; the car park at SU 646 715 is on the left.

More heaven-sent than devilish, Devil's Highway is the name given to the old Roman Road that heads west from London to Silchester (*Calleva*). Sadly no longer visible on the open road, this route crosses the old highway twice but the main attributes of the ride are the eclectic mix of smooth roads, canal crossings, motorway bridges and river crossings, which provide a stark contrast of old and new worlds colliding with each other. This is the perfect training ride for cadence and speed work that doesn't take up the whole day.

Overview
As the route heads off, Devil's Highway starts as it means to go on – flat! The navigation is straightforward enough and, except for one instance, is extremely well signposted. Arborfield Garrison is simple to navigate, and the river crossing soon after leaves no choice but to use the bridge. The only climbing involved is around Farley Hill and near the end.

1 Exit ➡ from the car park, continue along the High Street to the mini roundabout and turn ⬅ along Station Road. Go under the flyover and carry on ⬆ over two roundabouts. Cross over a canal bridge to reach a third roundabout, and turn ⬅ onto Deans Copse Road. Continue to a T-junction, turn L to go over the **M4**, and take the next ➡ onto Berrys Lane. Continue over a narrow railway bridge and back over the M4 along Hartley Court Road to a T-junction with Mereoak Lane.

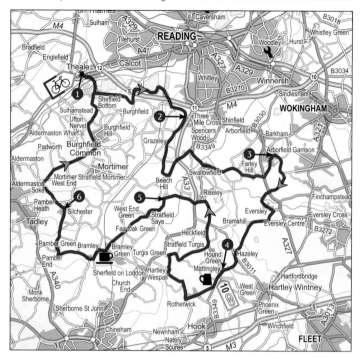

2   Turn → to reach a roundabout and take the second exit for Grazeley. As you leave **Grazeley** turn ← for Beech Hill. At a T-junction in **Beech Hill** turn ← for Spencers Wood, then turn → onto the **B3349** for 2km, and

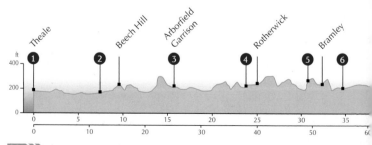

then turn ← for Swallowfield. Continue along this road through **Farley Hill** to the **A327**. Go ↑ onto Sheerlands Road to Arborfield Garrison. At the first T-junction in **Arborfield Garrison** turn →, then ← and turn → again at the roundabout in front of the barracks main gate to follow Biggs Lane and Park Lane.

3 Follow this road to the junction off Nine Mile Ride and turn → to continue along Park Lane to the A327 and go ↑ onto New Mill Road. Cross the ford using the bridge and continue to a small grass triangle junction with St Neot's Road and turn →. At the next junction turn → again onto Bramshill Road, then take the next ← along Plough Lane, signposted Hazeley. Continue to the **B3011** and turn ← and immediately → for Mattingley and Rotherwick.

Link to Route 10

If you've got some miles in your legs and you're looking for a bigger challenge, Devil's Highway links up nicely with The Hog's Back at **Mattingly**.

4 In **Mattingley** turn ← for Rotherwick to reach the B3349, then turn ← and take the second → for Rotherwick. At the T-junction at the far end of **Rotherwick** turn → onto Frog Lane and continue to the junction with Turgis Green Lane at **Hartley Wespall**. Turn → and continue to a T-junction, turn → again and then keep ← at the small green triangular junction and continue to the B3349. Turn

Berks on bike towards Arborfield

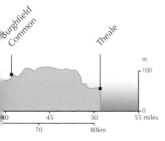

After Burghfield Common turn right for home

⬅ onto the **B3349** and continue to the second roundabout. Turn ⬅, signposted Reading, and go ⬆ at the roundabout over the A33 towards Mortimer.

5 At the T-junction in Fair Cross, turn ⬅ for Bramley, keep ➡ at the next junction and carry on past The Iron Duke after the crossroads in **Stratfield Saye**. Go ⬆ at a five-way junction to a T-junction in **Bramley**. Turn ➡ over railway lines, continue along Silchester Road (ignore the first junction for Silchester) to the junction with Little London and turn ➡ for Silchester.

6 In **Silchester**, turn ⬅ at the Calleva pub, then take the second ➡ for Aldermaston. At the roundabout take the second exit through Padworth Common to a roundabout in **Burghfield Common**. Turn ⬅ to reach traffic lights, and then turn ⬅ onto Hollybush Lane to a three-way junction and turn ➡ for Sulhamstead. At a crossroads at the bottom of the fast descent turn ⬅ to reach a roundabout. Turn ⬅ over the original canal bridge and continue past the railway station in **Theale**. Turn ➡ at the roundabout on the High Street and continue to return to the car park.

Route 10
The Hog's Back (Hampshire and Surrey)

Start/Finish	Hart Leisure Centre, Hitches Lane, Fleet SU 794 538
Distance	117km (73 miles)
Ascent	885m (2905ft)
Grade	
Time	5–6hrs 30mins
Feed stations	The Mill, Elstead; The Red Lion, Oakhanger
Access	From the centre of Fleet, follow the A323 past Calthorpe Park to a roundabout, and turn R onto Hitches Lane. Go SA at the next roundabout; Hart Leisure Centre at SU 794 538 is on the left.

The Hog's Back is another wonderful training ride that gets the miles in without the strain of big climbs. The climbing is cumulative rather than obvious, but the long climb up Brockham Hill out of Holybourne is worth a mention. It's a mixed bag of road surfaces and the difference between the two counties of Hampshire and Surrey is quite stark. There's no shortage of riders out and about either, so you won't be alone for long and catching riders ahead of you is a great way to train.

Overview

The initial run to Bentley is well signposted with an excellent descent to the A31. The terrain undulates from here on in until reaching the Hog's Back, but it's all good going. The return journey through Bordon and Oakhanger sees the return of some gentle hill work, but tired legs might feel otherwise. Old Basing offers some straightforward urban navigation, but the final few miles through Rotherwick, Dipley and Dogmersfield give a gentle flourish on which to finish this excellent ride.

1 Exit ← from the car park to a T-junction, and turn ← then first → onto Crondall Road. Turn ← onto the **A287** and then take the next → for Well and Crondall. Take the next ← for Crondall and continue through **Crondall** towards Well. After 2km turn ← for Bentley, then go ↑ at a crossroads to descend into **Bentley**.

2 Cross the **A31** onto Station Road to reach a crossroads at The Jolly Farmer pub at **Blacknest**. Turn ← onto Binsted Road to reach a

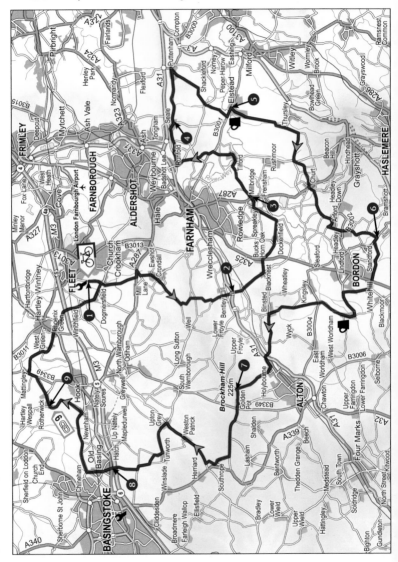

Warming up towards Bentley

T-junction with the **A325**, and turn ← then immediately → towards Dockenfield and Alice Holt Forest. At the bottom of the fast descent turn ← for **Dockenfield** (don't miss this!).

3 At the **A287** in **Millbridge** go ↑ onto Reeds Road to continue around a sharp ←↰ bend, and turn → for **Tilford**. Go over the **River Wey** and turn ← to reach a T-junction with the **B3001**. Turn ← then first → onto Crooksbury Road and continue to a T-junction with Guildford Road. Turn →, continue to a ←↰ bend and (carefully) turn → at the Hog's Back road sign towards Seale.

4 At the junction in **Seale** turn →, then keep ← for Puttenham. Turn → in **Puttenham** opposite The Good Intent pub onto Suffield Lane, pass between two lakes to reach a crossroads and go ↑ to a T-junction with the B3001. Turn ← for The Mill and Elstead.

5 Turn → at the green in **Elstead**, then → again and follow Thursley Road to a T-junction. Turn ← and go past the Pride of the Valley hotel and restaurant and turn → onto Hale House Lane. Continue to the A287 in **Churt** and go ↑ for Headley and Bordon. Keep ← on the Arford Road in

Turn left over the bridge in picturesque Tilford

Headley and climb to a junction with the **B3002**. Turn ➡ alongside the green, then take the first ⬅ onto Liphook Road.

6 Continue to a junction with the B3004, and turn ➡ then ⬅ onto Hollywater Road for Whitehill. Go ⬆ at the roundabout on the **A325**, then keep ➡ onto Hogmoor Road alongside the barracks and turn ⬅ onto Oakhanger Road. Swing north, passing the huge golf balls in

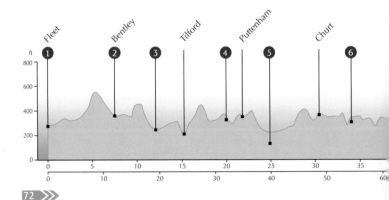

There is excellent signage through the narrow roads towards Weston Patrick

Oakhanger, to reach the **B3004**, and turn ← then immediately → for Binsted. Turn ← at **Binsted**, go under the **A31** and turn → (between two white houses) onto Church Lane in **Holybourne** to climb **Brockham Hill**.

7 At the top of the hill turn ← and go ↑ at the **B3349** towards Lasham Airfield. Turn → just before the entrance to the airfield onto Back Lane,

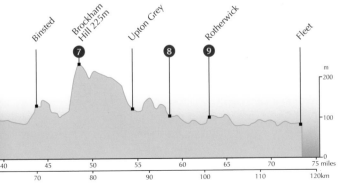

and keep → in **Southrope**, following signs for Weston Patrick. Turn → at the next T-junction, go through **Weston Patrick** to **Upton Grey** and turn ← next to the pond for **Tunworth**. Continue to Polecat Corner and turn → for Basing and Hatch.

8 Go over the **M3** and keep ↑ over the A30 into **Old Basing** to reach a five-way junction. Go ↑ onto Milkingpen Lane. Turn ← at the next junction then immediately turn → to follow Milkingpen Lane again. Continue to a T-junction and turn → past the Oliver's Battery and turn → onto Newham Lane. Turn ← in **Newham** onto Ridge Lane to reach Rotherwick.

Link to Route 9

If the legs are strong and the mind is willing, hit Devil's Highway at **Rotherwick** for extra stamina training.

9 Turn → onto The Street in **Rotherwick** and continue to the **B3349**. Turn ← then → for Dipley. On leaving Dipley turn → for Phoenix Green and go ↑ at the **A30** onto Dilly Lane. Turn → at the next T-junction, cross over the **M3** along Taplin's Lane and go ↑ at the crossroads towards Dogmersfield. Go through **Dogmersfield** and then turn ← onto Hitches Lane to return to the leisure centre.

Route 11
Mud, Sweat and Gears (Surrey)

Start/Finish	South Street car park, Godalming SU 968 437
Distance	85km (53 miles)
Ascent	1190m (3905ft)
Grade	
Time	3hrs 30mins–5hrs
Feed stations	The Noah's Ark Inn, Lurgashall; The Mucky Duck Inn, Tisman's Common
Access	From the edge of Godalming, pick up the A3100 (Flambard Way) Ring Road on the southern edge of town. The car park at SU 968 437 is behind the traffic lights, next to the junction for High Street and Holloway Hill.

Two climbs dominate this scenic and challenging Surrey route: the wooded, narrow ascent of Jay's and Tennyson's Lane near Haslemere, and the infamous Barnhatch Lane above Cranleigh. Arguably this is south east England's toughest climb, and it features regularly in major road races. But don't let this put you off: Mud, Sweat and Gears is as good as it gets when it comes to realistic yet challenging training rides.

Overview
Gentle rolling countryside features strongly on this route and the opening gambit out through Hambledon, Chiddingfold and Plaistow is a terrific warm up for the narrow, wooded climbs of Haslemere. The return journey also centres on rolling countryside and sweeping lanes, but save at least two chocolate bars for the approach to Cranleigh; Barnhatch Lane is pretty unforgiving if you're spent.

1 Exit the car park and turn ➡ onto the main road. At the traffic lights turn ⬅ onto Holloway Hill, continue to a road junction with Tuesley Lane and turn ⬅. Follow Tuesley Lane to a T-junction and turn ⬅. Continue to the crossroads at **Hydestile** and turn ➡ for Hambledon. As you enter **Hambledon**, turn ⬅ onto Woollands Road and continue to a T-junction. Turn ⬅ onto Vann Lane and continue to Chiddingfold.

2 At the T-junction in **Chiddingfold** turn ⬅ onto Pickhurst Road and continue towards Plaistow. Ignore the turning for High Street, and turn ➡

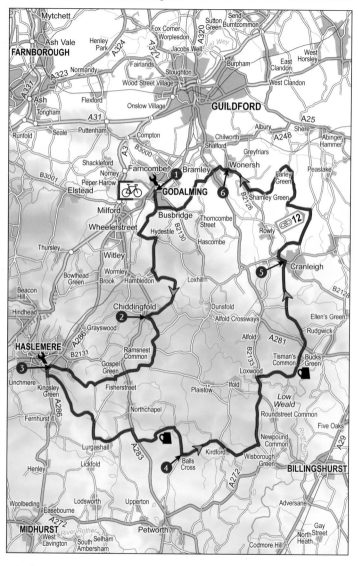

Leaving The Noah's Ark Inn, Lurgashall

at the next junction onto Shillinglee Park Road. Continue to a triangular junction and turn ➡. Squeeze between the two ponds to reach the **A283** and go ⬆ to Gospel Green. Turn ⬅ at Gospel Green and take the next ➡ onto Jay's Lane. Continue to the next junction, and turn ➡ to climb Tennyson's Lane. Descend to a T-junction and turn ➡ then take the next ⬅ onto Scotland Lane to descend into **Haslemere**.

3 Turn ⬅ onto the **A286** and take the second junction, turning ⬅ onto Fernden Lane. Continue to follow this narrow lane in its entirety as it

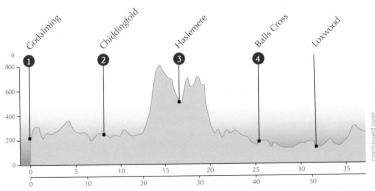

continued over

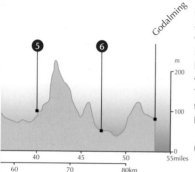

climbs and descends sharply to a T-junction at Quell Lane. Turn → for Dial Green then turn ← for Lurgashall. Just beyond the pub beside the green in **Lurgashall**, turn ← and continue to reach the A283. Turn → onto the **A283** and then take the next ← onto Streels Lane for Ebernoe and Balls Cross.

4 At the T-junction in **Balls Cross** turn ← and continue through **Kirdford** towards Wisborough Green. Just before entering **Wisborough Green** turn ← onto Skiff Lane for Loxwood. Turn ← onto the **B2133**, go over the **Wey and Avon Canal** and turn → onto Station Road, opposite the post office in **Loxwood**. At The Mucky Duck Inn in **Tisman's Common**, turn ← and continue to the A281. Go ↑ at the **A281** and continue along Knowle Lane to join the **B2128** at **Cranleigh**.

5 Turn ← onto the B2128 to reach a mini roundabout, and turn → past playing fields, following Horseshoe Lane to the junction with Amlets Lane. Turn → and continue to Barnhatch Lane. Turn ← to climb Barnhatch Lane.

Link to Route 12
If you really can't get enough of the hills around here, link this ride to Route 12 for permanent mental scarring. After climbing Barnhatch Lane go ↑ and drop into the village of **Shere** to join Surrey Hills.

Turn immediately ← on reaching the summit of Barnhatch Lane. Continue to a T-junction and turn → to descend into Farley Green. Turn ← in **Farley Green**, following Farley Heath Road to the junction with the B2128 at **Shamley Green**.

6 Follow the B2128 into **Wonersh** and turn ← onto The Street. Turn ← onto Station Road and go ↑ at the A281. Follow Snowdenham Lane to the junction with Iron Lane (Surrey Cycle Way) and turn →. Keep ← as you climb to reach the **B2130** and turn →. Continue to the churchyard and turn ← onto The Drive. At the junction with Tuesley Lane turn → and then → again to follow Tuesley Lane to a set of traffic lights. Turn → to return to South Street car park.

Route 12
Surrey Hills (Surrey)

Start/Finish	Pay and display car park opposite Headley Heath Cricket Pitch, TQ 205 539
Alternative Start/Finish	Box Hill pay and display car park TQ 179 513
Distance	90km (56 miles)
Ascent	1065m (3495ft)
Grade	
Time	3hrs 30mins–5hrs
Feed stations	Van at the start; The Six Bells, Newdigate; café atop Box Hill
Access	From Dorking, head east along the A25 towards Reigate to the roundabout at Betchworth and turn L up Station Road. Go over the railway line to the summit of the hill and turn L onto the B2033, signposted Leatherhead, Headley and Box Hill. Follow the road for a short distance until you reach the car park at TQ 205 539, which is on your left. If starting at Box Hill, take the first turning L after joining the B2033, signposted Box Hill, to reach the car park at TQ 179 513.

Here's a Jekyll and Hyde route if ever there was one. After a terrific circular warm-up ride, the Surrey Hills hit you, in all their glory, and it doesn't stop until the final turn of the pedal. However, you won't be alone; this is the stuff of Olympic and Tour of Britain road racing. Box Hill is the self-styled cycling playground of England's south east, but not just in the hilly parts. Here you'll find cyclists of all ages and abilities around the flatlands of Crawley, and rightly so; it's beautiful here, and whether you prefer the flatlands or the hills, it's simply superb riding.

Overview
The downhill opening leg and continuing flatland stretches help provide plenty of momentum to keep the wheels spinning all the way to Crawley. The return to Dorking is gentle on the legs – just as well too, as from here on in the contours come at you thick and fast. The final climb up Box Hill isn't as tough as some make out but, after all that's gone before, save something for a strong finish – all eyes will be watching from the café at the summit. Due to its popularity as a summit finish and café, Box Hill lends itself as an excellent alternative start/finish location.

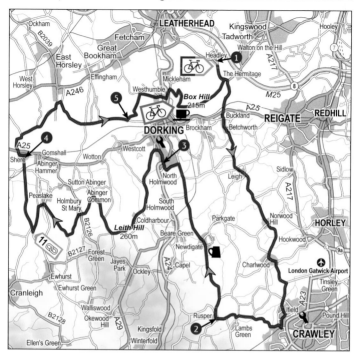

1 Exit → from the car park and descend to the B2032. (Carefully) turn →, continue down to the roundabout and go ↑. Turn ← at the next T-junction, then take the next → onto The Street. At the next T-junction, turn ← to go through **Leigh** along Smalls Hill Road to a T-junction at **Charlwood**. Turn ← then → opposite the Rising Sun onto Ifield Road. On the approach

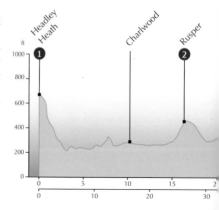

Climbing Combe Lane – too painful to appreciate the beauty

to Crawley, turn ➜ onto Ifield Green opposite a tall telephone mast, continue into **Ifield** and turn ➜ at the Langley Corner Surgery onto Rusper Road. Continue to a T-junction and turn ➜ into **Rusper**.

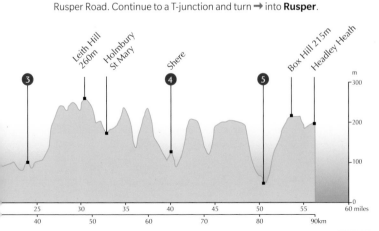

2 Continue through Rusper and head for Newdigate. On exiting **Newdigate** turn ← onto Henfold Lane for Dorking, continue under the railway line along Blackbrook Road to the junction with Inholms Lane and turn ←. At the T-junction with Spook Hill turn → to the busy round-about and go ↑ to the **A24**.

3 Climb Flint Hill as far as the junction with Knoll Road, turn ← to continue to the junction with Coldharbour Lane and turn ←. Follow the narrow confines of Coldharbour Lane past **Coldharbour Common** and keep → to follow the signs for Leith Hill. Keep → beyond **Leith Hill** and descend Leith Hill Road towards **Abinger Common**. At the bottom of Leith Hill Road turn ← onto Pasture Wood Road for **Holmbury St Mary** to the junction with the **B2126** and turn → then immediately ← along Pitland Street to climb Holmbury Hill to a T-junction. Turn → for Peaslake. Go ↑ at the junction with the cross in **Peaslake**, go ← past The Hurtwood Inn and climb Walking Bottom Lane. At the junction at the top turn → onto Hound House Lane (very narrow) to descend into Shere.

Link to Route 11
After climbing out of **Peaslake** and turning → at the top, link Surrey Hills to Mud, Sweat and Gears for the ride of your life by taking the next ← onto Barnhatch Lane. Turn → before descending the steep hill (it's a long slog back up) and follow the lane to Farley Green.

4 Turn ← in **Shere** and follow Upper Street to the **A25**. Turn → then immediately ← up Combe Lane. Keep → at the top and follow the long descent to the junction with Crocknorth Road. Turn sharp → uphill and follow the ridge road to Ranmore Common. Turn ← down the singletrack lane, next to the white cottage, signposted Bookham and Westhumble.

5 Descend to the T-junction, turn → and continue to reach the **A24**. Turn ← onto the main road, get into the ⤵ lane and take the second exit off the roundabout for Box Hill. Follow the brown signposts and turn → for **Box Hill**. Climb Zig-Zag Road past the café and car park (an alternative start/finish point) to the road junction beyond Box Hill village. Turn ← onto the B2033 and climb to the second car park on the ←.

Route 13
Reservoir Cogs (Surrey and Sussex)

Start/Finish	Gloucester Road car park, Redhill TQ 279 509
Distance	101km (63 miles)
Ascent	1420m (4660ft)
Grade	▲▲▲
Time	4–6hrs
Feed stations	Java & Jazz Café, Forest Row
Access	The main artery running through Redhill is the A23. At the roundabout at the end of the Princess Way leg of the A23, near the town centre, go SA onto Gloucester Road to reach the car park at TQ 279 50, which is on your right.

Reservoir Cogs has arguably the finest opening section of any route in this book. The first 15 miles or so has so much packed into it, it's like a mini sportive in itself; just don't overcook too early. There are plenty of great hills to climb; most notably White Hill, Succomb's Lane and Cobb Lane. Stunning scenery is viewed from every high point, if you can lift your head from your chest. A clear set of lungs and a fresh pair of legs are highly recommended for this ride.

Overview

Climbing stamps its mark on this route from the moment you get on the pedals, but flatteringly fast stretches help eat up the miles high above Redhill and Caterham; they can also lead the unwary into a false sense of security. Once Succomb's Lane is conquered the route eases back and you'll find the roads to Lingfield and Forest Row offer low resistance. However, after nearly 40 miles, Cobb Lane is unforgiving and Ardingly feels remote; you'll find 'Reservoir Cogs' lives up to its name.

1 Exit the car park, turn → onto Gloucester Road, continue to the junction with Linkfield Lane and turn →. Take the next ← onto **Daneshill** and go ↑ at the crossroads onto Coniston Way. Turn ← onto Batts Hill, past the Windmill, to reach the roundabout on the A242, and go ↑ to climb Wray Lane. At the awkward double junction at the top turn → onto Gatton Bottom and continue to the junction with the A23.

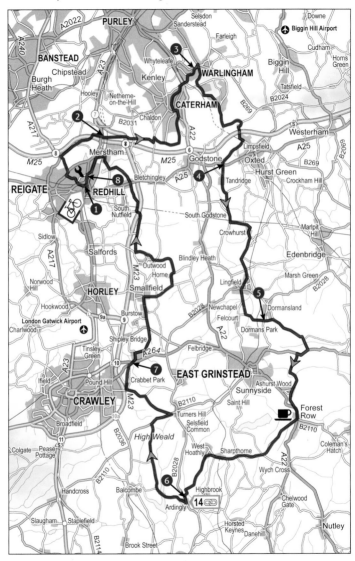

Succomb's Hill – cars stall, as do legs

2 Go ↑ at the A23 onto Rockshaw Road, continue over the **M25** and carry on to a T-junction. Turn ← then → onto Spring Bottom Lane. Continue to a T-junction with Whitehill Lane and turn ← uphill. Turn → at the top onto War Coppice Road, continue to a T-junction and turn ← onto Tupwood Lane. Follow this into **Caterham** to a junction with Godstone Road and turn ←. At a roundabout turn ← and then turn → after the station onto Stafford Road and continue to a T-junction. Turn → to reach the roundabout on the **A22** and take the second exit. Climb Succomb's Hill and continue to the junction with the B270 (Westhall Road).

3 Turn → onto Westhall Road, then → at the green onto Redvers Road, then → again onto Leas Road. Descend Bug Hill to a four-way junction and take the second ← onto Woldingham Road. Carry on uphill past the station into Woldingham along Northdown Road. Continue on, as the road swings ← along the Ridge, and turn → down Chalkpit Lane to go under the M25 and the railway arch to reach the junction with Barrow Green Road. Turn → to the roundabout on the **A25**.

4 Go ↑ along Tandridge Lane to a T-junction and turn →. Carry on to the railway bridge and turn ← onto Crowhurst Lane. Continue to a dog-leg junction, go ↑ to follow Crowhurst Lane into **Lingfield** and turn →

Homeward bound – the windmill near Outwood

onto Saxbys Lane. Continue to the **B2028** (High Street) and turn ➜ to reach a roundabout. Turn ⬅ onto East Grinstead Road and ⬅ at the end of the racecourse onto Blackberry Lane, keeping ⬅ again to stay on Blackberry Lane to go past a golf course and a railway station to a crossroads.

5 Go ⬆ onto Mutton Hill, then turn ➜ onto Hollow Lane and continue to the A264 and turn ➜. Carry on through woods to the first junction, turn ⬅ onto Shovelstrode Lane and continue to a T-junction in **Ashurst Wood**. Turn ➜ then ⬅ at

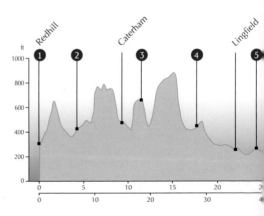

the next T-junction onto Wall Hill Road and turn ← to join the **A22** into **Forest Row**. At a mini roundabout in front of the church turn → onto Priory Road, continue to **Sharpthorne** and turn ← onto Church Hill for West Hoathly. Follow the road ← through **West Hoathly** to descend Hook Lane and then climb Cobb Lane to join the **B2028**.

Link to Route 14
If you've got the stamina and the time, **Ardingly** is the link in the chain to Park and Ride if you fancy dipping your toes in the sea.

6 Turn ← into **Ardingly** then → into Street Lane and → again to follow Street Lane down to the reservoir. Go across the causeway and turn → up Paddockhurst Lane to the **B2110**. Turn → onto the B2110 then ← at Turners Hill, signposted Worth and Crawley, but, before going over the M23, turn → onto Old Hollow at a brown signpost for the Regency Hotel. This continues towards Copthorne, reaching a T-junction with the A2220. Here turn → to a roundabout on the **A264**.

7 Go ↑ at the roundabout onto Brookhill Road then turn → at The Prince Albert pub onto Copthorne Bank. Go ↑ at the B2037 to **Smallfield** and turn → just before the mini roundabout onto New Road. Turn → again at the end of the road, then ← onto Plough Road. Continue to Church Lane and turn ←, signposted Horne and Godstone. Take the next ← onto Horne Court Hill to the windmill at **Outwood** and turn ←. Turn immediately → onto Millers Lane, then → again onto Brickfield Road.

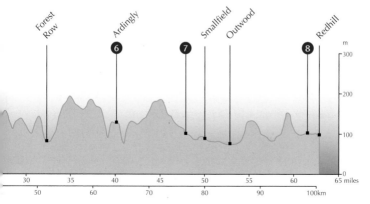

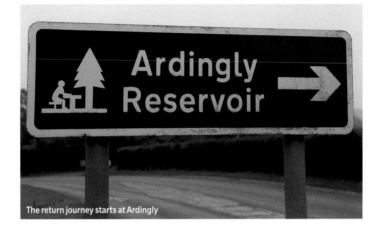

The return journey starts at Ardingly

Continue to a T-junction and turn ➡. Carry on under the **M23**, then go ⬆ at the A25 into **Redhill**.

8 Turn ⬅ at the roundabout next to the church onto Battlebridge Lane and continue to a T-junction. Turn ⬅ then immediately ➡ onto Frenches Road. At the roundabout go ⬆ to the A23, turn ⬅ then ➡ at the roundabout into Gloucester Road and turn ➡ to return to the car park.

Route 14
Park and Ride (East Sussex)

Start/Finish	Withdean Sports Complex car park TQ 297 076
Distance	100km (62 miles)
Ascent	1410m (4625ft)
Grade	
Time	4–6hrs
Feed stations	Café/restaurant at start; The Hatch Inn, Colemans Hatch
Access	From the centre of Brighton follow the A23 (London Road) north to the junction with Tongdean Lane, which has a large signpost for 'Withdean Sports Complex'. Turn L and go under the railway line to a T-junction. Turn R and follow the road around to the L and into the car park at TQ 297 076.

Some of the best riding that England's south coast and the Weald have to offer can be found on this stunning and challenging ride. Classic climbs such as Kidds Hill and Ditchling Beacon supplement the beautiful rolling countryside of this ever-popular sportive cycling area. Well surfaced roads feature strongly too and offer excellent opportunities to up the cadence, while the big climbs favour those riders who've put the training miles in first. Ashdown Forest alone is stunning and worth the trip, as is the challenge of Kidds Hill.

Overview

After the start, with a long gentle climb up to Devil's Dyke, contours don't feature too strongly as the route heads towards Haywards Heath and the miles are soon eaten up. Things tend to get a little lumpier around Ardingly, but Ashdown Forest and Kidds Hill are pure joy. The riding is as smooth as honey past the home of Winnie the Pooh, but then the taxing question of Ditchling Beacon arises – always a test of both stamina and character.

1 Exit ← from the car park and follow Tongdean Lane up to the T-junction with Dyke Road, turn → and go over the two roundabouts onto Devil's Dyke Road. Keep ← for Devil's Dyke, follow the road around and down to a T-junction and turn ←. At the bottom of the hill turn sharp ← onto Poynings Road, continue to a sharp ↰ bend in **Fulking** and turn →

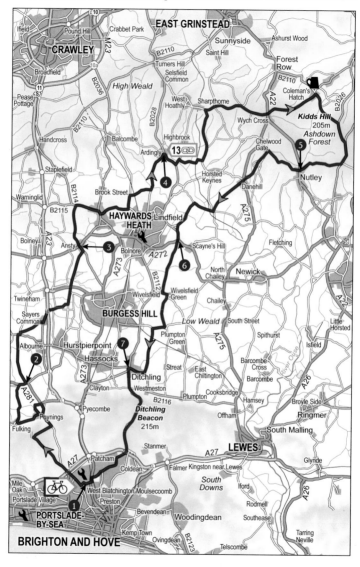

Along Mill Lane and then over the A23

onto Clappers Lane. At the junction with the **A281** turn ➜ and take the next ← onto Shaves Wood Lane.

2 Continue to the B2116 and turn ➜ then ←, and immediately ➜ onto Reed's Lane. At **Sayers Common** turn ← onto the B2118, then go ➜ at the next roundabout onto Mill Lane, then go ➜ again to continue along Mill Lane. At the T-junction with Cuckfield Road turn ←, continue to the roundabout with the A2300 and go ↑ to join the B2036. Turn ← for Ansty to reach the roundabout on the **A272** in **Ansty**. Turn ← then immediately ➜ down Deak's Lane.

3 Continue to the **B2115**. Turn ➜ for Whitemans Green, turn ➜ again at the roundabout with the B2036, then go ← at the next roundabout onto Ardingly Road. Continue to a T-junction and turn ←. As the road descends past an old brick building on the ←, turn ➜ onto Copyhold Lane, signposted Ardingly. At the next junction turn ← for Ardingly.

Don't miss the train

Link to Route 13

Turn ← onto Street Lane in **Ardingly** to totally blow your legs and mind as you link up with Reservoir Cogs. But beware: Succomb's Hill and Cobb Lane will take no prisoners.

4 Turn → onto the **B2028** in **Ardingly**, then turn ← onto Burstow Hill Lane, signposted Highbrook and West Hoathly. Take the next → onto Station Approach to the junction with Cider Hill Lane and turn ← for Sharpthorne. At the T-junction in **Sharpthorne** turn →, continue to a crossroads and turn → for **Wych Cross** and the junction

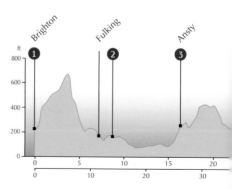

with the A22. Go ⬆ at the **A22** into **Ashdown Forest** and continue to Coleman's Hatch. As you approach **Coleman's Hatch** turn ➡ at the green, then ➡ again past the Hatch Inn to descend then climb **Kidds Hill**. At the junction with the **B2026** turn ➡, continue across the high ridge, then turn ➡ at Camp Hill onto Crowborough Road, signposted Nutley.

5 On reaching the **A22** turn ⬅ uphill, then carefully turn sharp ➡, signposted Chelwood Gate. At **Chelwood Gate** turn ⬅ onto Stone Quarry Road, signposted Chelwood Common, and continue to **Danehill** and the junction with the A275. Turn ⬅ onto the **A275** then turn ➡ as the road bends ⬅ onto Freshfield Lane. Continue to Freshfield Crossways and turn ➡, signposted Haywards Heath and Lindfield Golf Club. At the T-junction with the B2111, turn ⬅ to reach the **A272**. Turn ➡ then ⬅ onto Slugwash Lane.

6 Follow the lane to the T-junction in **Wivelsfield** and turn ⬅, then take the next ➡ onto South Road and go ➡ again at a mini roundabout onto Hundred Acre Lane (whispered Piglet). Go past Hundred Acre Wood on the ⬅ to the T-junction with Middle Common Lane and turn ➡. At a sharp ↱ bend turn ⬅ onto Spatham Lane, go across the railway line and continue to the B2116. Turn ⬅ towards Ditchling.

7 At the roundabout in **Ditchling**, turn ⬅ onto the B2112, then turn ⬅ again onto Beacon Road, signposted Ditchling Beacon, climbing then

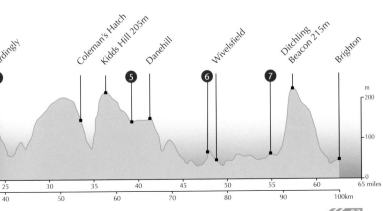

Head for Haywards Heath from Freshfield Crossways

descending **Ditchling Beacon** to a T-junction above the A27. Turn
→ to reach the roundabout, turn ← over the **A27**, then take the second ← off the next roundabout onto Carden Avenue. Follow Carden
Avenue down to the **A23**, and turn ← then immediately → onto The
Deneway. Go under the railway bridge, turn ← at a Y-junction and go
← again onto Eldred Avenue. Continue to a T-junction and turn → onto
Tongdean Lane to return to the car park on the ←.

Route 15
Weald-a-Beast (Kent)

Start/Finish	Sevenoaks swimming centre long stay car park TQ 533 548
Alt Start/Finish	Penshurst Station TQ 519 465
Distance	92km (57 miles)
Ascent	1170m (3840ft)
Grade	
Time	3hrs 30mins–5hrs
Feed stations	Costa, High Street, West Malling; Abergavenny Arms, Frant; Fir Tree Tea Rooms, Penshurst
Access	Head into Sevenoaks town centre via the A224, turn onto High Street and follow the road to the traffic lights at the crossroads. Turn R into Suffolk Way and continue into the far end of the long stay car park at TQ 533 548.

To call Weald-a-Beast an 'undulating' route would be a foolish understatement. The stunning countryside throughout the Low and High Weald of Kent offers little in the way of an easy ride. Climbs and descents of varying lengths and severity offer little respite or recuperation with the idea of fast cadence training best left for a different route. At 50 miles into the ride, Toy's Hill is a real test at any level, so the inclusion of the alternate start/finish from Penshurst Station gives riders the opportunity to conquer this classic climb with fresh legs and a train ride to boot.

Overview

Sevenoaks is soon left behind after a quick descent, and the run out through Plaxtol and West Malling provides a gentle taste of things to come. Contours begin to close-up around Brenchley and Frant as the High Weald kicks in. After Penshurst, the ridge that hosts Toy's Hill looms large and tension mounts. With climbing far from over, the roller-coaster ride from Goathurst Common precedes a fabulously long freewheel back towards the centre of Sevenoaks – and a final reminder of just how tough this classic training ride is.

1 Exit the car park and continue to the traffic lights. Turn ➡ then ➡ again and descend the B2019 to the turning at the bottom of the hill and turn ➡ for Godden Green. At the junction in Godden Green turn ➡, continue to a crossroads and turn ⬅ for **Stone Street**. Turn ➡ at Stone

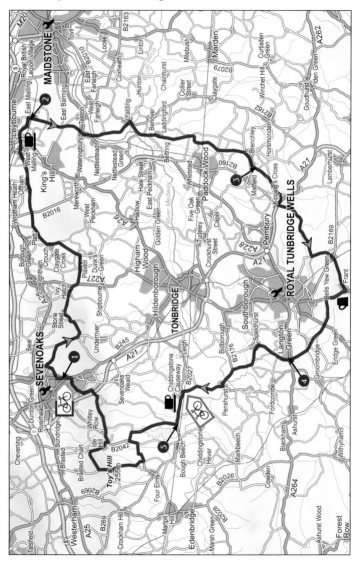

Street, carry on through **Ivy Hatch** to the **A227** and take the next ← for Plaxtol. As you descend through **Plaxtol** turn ← for Crouch. At the bottom of the descent out of **Crouch** turn → onto Beechin Wood Lane and continue to the **B2016**. Go ↑ into **Offham** and turn → for West Malling. Turn ← at the next turning into **West Malling** and continue to the High Street. Turn ← onto the High Street and immediately turn → to go under the railway line and the A228 to head towards East Malling.

Turn right for High Rocks and tall hills

2 At the crossroads in the centre of **East Malling** turn → and continue to the A26 at **Wateringbury**. Go ↑ onto the B2015 and turn sharp ← at the bottom of the descent to cross the River Medway and head for Yalding. Turn → at the crossroads in **Yalding**, cross the narrow bridge and turn → onto the B2162. Take the next turning → for Paddock Wood and Laddingford. Turn → opposite the school in **Laddingford** and continue along this road to climb into Brenchley (ignore the left turn for Brenchley

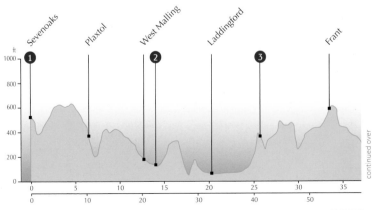

after Queen Street). Turn ➜ in **Brenchley**, then ➜ again at a T-junction. Turn ⬅ just past Brenchley Garage to descend Petteridge Lane.

3 Turn ➜ at the T-junction at Old Cryals and continue to the **A21**. Carefully turn ➜ to the second roundabout, turn ⬅ onto Dundale Road and continue to Kippling's Cross. Turn ⬅ for Bells Yew Green and Frant. Go ⬆ at the **B2169** at Frant Station and continue to the A267 in **Frant**. Turn ➜, descend along the main road and turn ⬅ onto Bunny Lane, signposted Groombridge. Go ⬆ at the A26 then turn ➜, signposted High Rocks. Keep ⬅ at the next junction and continue to a crossroads. Go ⬆ under the railway bridge and climb to the A264 at **Langton Green**.

4 Go ⬆ at the **A264** onto The Green and continue to **Speldhurst**. Turn ⬅ at a T-junction, continue to the **B2176** and turn ⬅ for Penshurst. In the centre of **Penshurst** turn ➜ onto the B2176 and climb past Penshurst Park. Turn ⬅ to follow the B2176 down towards Penshurst Station (an alternative start/finish point). Continue on the B2176, turn ⬅ to follow the B2027 to a short rise in the road and turn ➜ at the brown signpost for Bough Beech Reservoir and Reserve.

5 Take the next ⬅, signposted Winkhurst Green and Ide Hill, and continue to the **B2042**. Turn ⬅, continue to the crossroads at Piggott's Cross and turn ➜ for **Toy's Hill**. At the top of the climb, turn ➜ just past the pub onto Emmetts Lane and descend to a T-junction. Turn ➜ and climb to **Ide Hill**. Turn ⬅ at the junction in the village and descend to

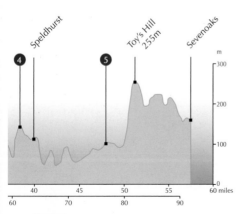

the B4042. Turn ⬅, climb to Goathurst Common and turn ➜, signposted Sevenoaks. Continue to a T-junction, turn ⬅ over the **A21** then turn ⬅ again to freewheel into **Sevenoaks**. At the T-junction with the A225, turn ⬅ then turn ➜ in front of HSBC Bank to reach traffic lights. Turn ➜ to return to the swimming centre car park.

Route 16
Battle Plan (Sussex and Kent)

Start/Finish	Sovereign Centre car park, Eastbourne TQ 632 006
Distance	90km (56 miles)
Ascent	970m (3180ft)
Grade	
Time	3hrs–4hrs 30mins
Feed stations	Benji's Coffee Shop, Market Square, Battle; The Swan Inn, Wood's Corner; Polegate Café, Polegate
Access	The car park at TQ 632 006 is found at the northern end of 'Royal Parade' on the seafront. An alternative is to follow the A22 to the final large roundabout, turn L onto Lottbridge Dove and go SA at two roundabouts to reach the seafront. Here you will find the car park right in front of you.

All good battle plans require flexibility, and this classic training ride has plenty of options for change. The excellent road layout here provides riders with an endless supply of training options – Battle Plan only scratches the surface. It is a route that's simple to navigate and yet still manages to capture all that is special to this area: Norman's Bay (1066 and all that), the Pevensey Levels, Beachy Head and a spectacular sweeping descent into Eastbourne that will leave you grinning for weeks.

Overview

Warm ups don't come much flatter than the run out to the shingle of Norman's Bay, but that's where it ends. The contours squeeze up through Henley's Down, Crowhurst and Battle, and the long climb up to Netherfield affords some stunning views back towards the coast. The unique and slightly eerie feeling of the Pevensey Levels brings some welcome relief before the climbing starts again after Polegate, which includes the classic but easily achievable prize of Beachy Head.

1 Exit the car park, take the fourth exit off the roundabout, signposted Pevensey Bay, and go ⬆ at the next roundabout onto the **B2104**. Turn ➡ after the roundabout onto Priory Road and keep ➡ to stay on Priory Road. Continue to the roundabout on the B2191. Turn ➡, continue through **Pevensey** to the A259 and turn ⬅ to the roundabout. Take the

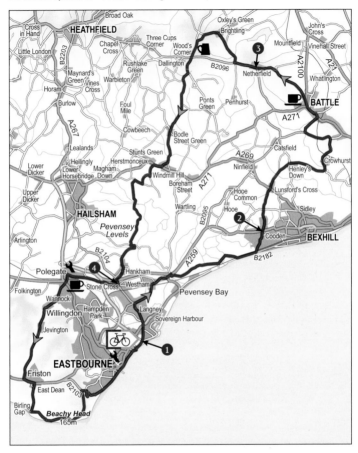

fourth exit for Norman's Bay, continue to the junction with the **B2182** on the edge of **Bexhill** and turn ← to the roundabout on the **A259**.

2 Go ↑ at the roundabout, continue to the **A269** and turn ← then immediately → onto Watermill Lane. Continue to the junction in **Henley's Down** and turn → for Crowhurst. Keep ← on the steep descent, signposted Battle, climb up past the railway station in **Crowhurst** to the

Stormin' Norman's Bay

junction with Telham Lane and turn ← to continue to the **B2095**. Turn → and climb to the A2100 and then turn ← into **Battle**. At the roundabout, follow the **A2100** out of Battle, signposted Sevenoaks. Continue for a short distance, turn ← onto Netherfield Road and continue to the **B2096** at **Netherfield**.

3 Turn →, descend to a small crossroads and turn → for Brightling. Keep ← in **Brightling**, then go ← again at the end of the park to return to the B2096 at **Wood's Corner**. Go ↑, descend to a three-way junction and turn → for Bodle Street Green. Continue through **Bodle Street**

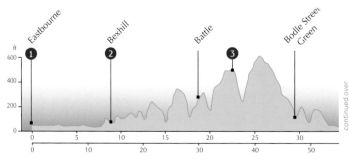

continued over

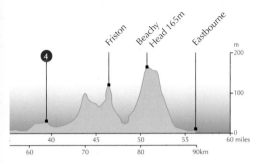

Green to the **A271** at **Windmill Hill**. Turn ➡ then take the next ⬅ for Flowers Green. Turn ➡ onto Butler's Lane, then turn ➡ at the T-junction next to the small junction and turn ⬅ for Rickney. At the T-junction in Rickney turn ⬅ then take the next ➡ for **Hankham** and continue to the **B2104** at **Stone Cross**.

4 Turn ⬅ then take the next ➡ onto the B2247 and go ⬆ at the roundabout on the A22 into **Polegate**. Turn ⬅ for the railway station next to Kontour Cycles and continue through **Wannock** and **Jevington** to the A259 at **Friston**. Turn ⬅ to descend to the junction at the bottom of the steep hill then turn ➡ for **Birling Gap**. Follow the road around and climb to **Beachy Head** and the junction with the **B2103**. Turn ➡ then immediately ➡ again, signposted seafront, and descend into **Eastbourne**. Follow the seafront road all the way back to the Sovereign Centre car park.

The view to Beachy Head

Route 17
Merry Wives (Bucks and Berkshire)

Start/Finish	Oxford Road car park, Marlow SU 847 866
Distance	60km (37 miles)
Ascent	540m (1770ft)
Grade	▲
Time	2hrs 15mins–3hrs 30mins
Feed stations	Cafés on the High Street, Marlow; Costa, Eton
Access	Leave the A404 to join the A4155 to the east of Marlow and head into the town centre. On reaching the mini roundabout at the head of High Street opposite Costa Coffee, go SA and take the next turning R, onto Oxford Road. The car park at SU 847 866 is on your right.

Perfectly placed to the west of London, Merry Wives offers easy access to some superb open countryside. Short, sharp, quirky and interesting, this route has the all right ingredients for a delightful ride. Navigation is straightforward around Eton and Windsor and the route is well signposted; you can't miss the castle as a reference point either. Speed and cadence training opportunities are plentiful here and some great descents are to be found after the few relatively short climbs involved.

Overview
A couple of steady climbs warm the legs before the excellent flat sections high above the Thames squeeze quietly between Maidenhead and Slough. Head over the bridge in Eton, climb past the castle and wiggle your way west out towards White Waltham before heading up past Maidenhead and Marlow for an exciting and picturesque finish over the Thames.

 Exit ← from the car park, turn ← again to a roundabout and go ↑. Turn → at the next roundabout, continue to the junction with Marlow Road and turn ←, signposted Marlow Bottom. Turn ← at another roundabout, climb to the top of the hill and turn → onto the singletrack road to descend Winchbottom Lane. Turn ← at the three-way junction in the valley floor and climb to the T-junction with Heath End Road. Turn → for **Flackwell Heath** and Wooburn Green.

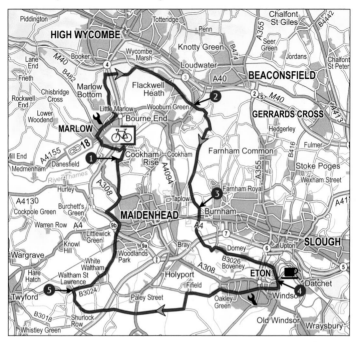

2 Entering **Wooburn Green**, turn ← onto the **A4094** then immediately
→ beside The Green. Continue → around The Green, turning ← just
past the Red Cow Pub up Windsor Hill. Turn → at the top of the hill onto
Broad Lane, then ← onto Wooburn Common Road, signposted Taplow.

Turn → onto Sheepcote
Lane at the junction in
the tree line, signposted
Taplow. Continue to the
T-junction with Heathfield
Road and turn →. Keep
→ past The Feathers pub
along Cliveden Road to
reach a road junction with
Hill Farm Road (tiny grass
triangle) and turn ←.

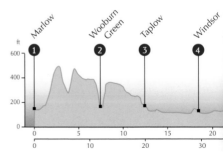

Pancake flat and perfect pedalling

3 Continue along the edge of **Taplow** to Station Road and turn ➡ just before the white gates, signposted Maidenhead. Go under the railway arches to the **A4** and go ⬆ at the lights onto Marsh Lane. Continue over the M4 to the **B3026** and turn ➡ through **Dorney** to reach Eton Wick and a T-junction opposite Eton College Chapel. Turn ➡ onto the High Street and continue to the traffic-free bridge. Turn ⬅ over the River Thames into **Windsor**.

4 Go ⬆ at the crossroads, up past the castle to traffic lights and turn ➡ onto Victoria Street. Go ⬆ at the large, busy roundabout on the A332

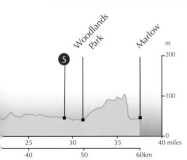

along the Dedworth Road and ⬆ at two cuff linked roundabouts to a T-junction. Turn ⬅ onto the **B3024** to join Oakley Green Road, then turn ⬅ at a crossroads onto Fifield Lane. Continue to a T-junction and turn ➡. Follow Drift Road over two roundabouts and the **M4** to Beenham's Heath. Turn ➡, signposted Waltham St Lawrence, and continue to the **B3024**.

Marlow Bridge – what a finish line

5 Turn ➡ and keep ⬅ into **White Waltham**. At the roundabout in **Woodlands Park** turn ⬅ onto Cannon Lane and go under the railway line and the **M404** flyover to a roundabout. Go ⬆ onto Henley Road and then take the next ➡ onto Pinkneys Drive, signposted Pinkneys Green, to the A308. Turn ⬅ onto the **A308** then ➡ up Winter Hill Road, and continue to the junction with Quarry Wood Road. Turn ⬅ downhill, go under the A404 and turn ➡ to go over the River Thames into **Marlow** and onto the High Street. At the end of the High Street, turn ⬅ then ➡ onto Oxford Road to return to the car park.

Link to Route 18
Marlow links Merry Wives and the Wycombe Wanderer if it's an epic day in the saddle that you're after – chalk and cheese comes to mind.

Route 18
The Wycombe Wanderer (Bucks and Oxon)

Start/Finish	Dean Street car park, Marlow SU 849 868
Distance	106km (66 miles); via shortcut: 72km (45 miles)
Ascent	1410m (4625ft)
Grade	▲▲▲
Time	4hrs 30mins–6hrs; via shortcut: 3hrs–4hrs
Feed stations	Cafés in Marlow; Rumsey's Chocolaterie and Whitewaters Café, Wendover; Roald Dahl Museum Café, Great Missenden
Access	Leave the A404 to join the A4155 to the east of Marlow and head into the town centre. As you reach the red-bricked Waitrose building, turn R at the roundabout and turn R again into the car park at SU 849 868.

The Chilterns are one of the finest cycling locations you could ever wish for and are as picturesque as they are challenging. Mile upon mile of rolling countryside peppered with classic climbs await your pleasure: Chinnor, Whiteleaf, Wendover Hill and Abbey Barn Lane. But with plenty of good going in between, there's ample opportunity to ease off on the lactic and catch your breath. Long climbs usually mean long sweeping descents and the Chilterns don't disappoint here either. If you stop for a brew mid-ride, check out the Roald Dahl Museum Café for all its wicked wackiness.

Overview
The route starts with a long, undulating climb up to Christmas Common – a perfect warm-up – and the theme continues as the route cuts in and out of the Chilterns' classic, steep escarpment towards Princes Risborough. With a rest from the hills after Wendover, the route into Chesham and Great Missenden offers a welcome respite, before things get much lumpier again towards the end.

 Exit ← out of the car park and turn → at the roundabout. Turn → at the next roundabout onto West Street, then → again and follow Oxford Road to the crossroads at **Frieth**. Go ↑ and turn ← at the next junction towards Fingest. Turn → in **Fingest**, signposted Turvile, follow Holloway Lane to the junction in **Northend** and turn →. At the junction in **Christmas Common** turn →, go past a very large radio tower and continue over the **M40** to the junction with the A40.

Even in the mist the radio tower is quite an impressive marker – no signal though!

2 Carefully go ↑ at the **A40**, descend Kingston Hill to the **B4009** and turn → into **Chinnor**. At the mini roundabout, turn → onto Station Road, signposted Bledlow Ridge, and climb Chinnor Hill. Just after the steepest section, turn ←, signposted Bledlow Ridge. After a short

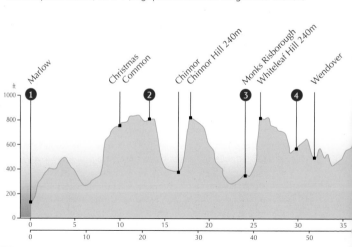

At Buckland Common go right to follow NCN 30 into Chesham

stretch of high ground, turn ← onto Wigans Lane, signposted Bledlow and Princes Risborough, descending to the B4009 once again. Turn → and go under a railway arch, keeping →, to reach the roundabout at Longwick. Go ↑.

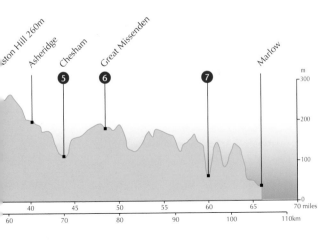

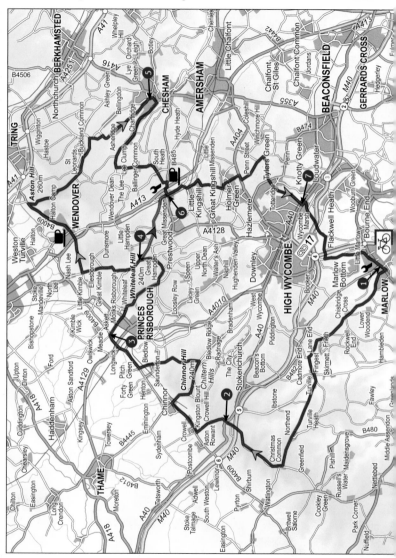

The penultimate climb up Abbey Barn Lane – tears may be shed

3 Take the next turning → onto Mill Lane for **Monks Risborough**, go under the railway bridge to the A4010 and turn → then immediately ← onto Peters Lane, signposted Hampden and Whiteleaf Hill. Go up **Whiteleaf Hill** to the T-junction at Redland End and then turn ← onto Pink Road. Keep ← through **Great Hampden** to the crossroads, turn ← onto Hampden Road and continue to a T-junction.

Shortcut to Great Missenden
If you're having a bad day, turn → at this T-junction to pick up the route again in **Great Missenden**.

4 Turn ← at the T-junction, go past Chequers to the crossroads at Butler's Cross and turn → to continue into **Wendover**. Turn → at the second roundabout at the end of the High Street, signposted Tring, and go past RAF Halton to the junction for Aston Hill, St Leonards and Buckland Common. Climb the hill and continue to the sharp ← bend beyond **St Leonards** and turn → onto Oak Lane, signposted Braziers End (National Cycle Network 30). At the triangular junction in Braziers End turn → to follow Braziers End Lane, then → again to follow the NCN 30 through **Asheridge** into Chesham.

5 At the T-junction in **Chesham** turn → to just past the large mosque and then turn → again onto Lowndes Avenue. Continue to the double T-junction and turn → onto Chartridge Lane. Follow this out through **Chartridge** to a road junction, signposted Lee Common, and turn ← for Ballinger. Continue to the **B485** at Frith Hill and turn → to reach the roundabout on the **A413**. Turn → then ← at the next roundabout into **Great Missenden**.

6 At the mini roundabout turn ← onto the High Street, pass the Roald Dahl Museum and continue to the junction with Nag's Head Lane. Turn → and go under the railway bridge. Turn ← onto Windsor Lane, climb to the junction with Watchet Lane and turn ←, signposted **Holmer Green**. Continue to the roundabout, turn ← then → onto New Pond Road, go ↑ at the crossroads to the **A404** and turn →. Take the next ← along Gravelly Way, signposted Penn Bottom. At the end of the wood line turn → onto Common Wood Lane to reach the **B474**. Go ↑ onto New Road and continue as the road narrows along Cock Lane to descend to the A40.

7 Turn ← at the lights onto the **A40** and then immediately turn → at the next lights onto Abbey Barn Lane. Continue to the sharp ↰ bend and carefully turn → up Abbey Barn Lane. Carry on under the **M40** to a T-junction.

Link to Route 17

Need a longer warm-down? At the junction turn ← for **Flackwell Heath** to join Merry Wives.

For the main route, turn → at the junction. Turn immediately ← onto Winchbottom Lane, turn → at the bottom and climb to the T-junction. Turn ← and descend towards **Marlow**. At the roundabout turn → onto Wycombe Road and continue to a T-junction. Turn → to reach a roundabout and turn → again to return to Dean Street car park.

Route 19
Oxtail Loop (Oxfordshire)

Start/Finish	Kidlington Leisure Centre, Oxford SP 496 132
Distance	68km (42 miles)
Ascent	430m (1410ft)
Grade	▲
Time	2hrs 30mins–4hrs
Feed stations	The Duke of Marlborough, nr Woodstock; The Fox Inn, Leafield
Access	From the centre of Oxford, take the A4165 (Banbury Road) north to cross over the A34. At the large roundabout, go SA to follow the road into Kidlington. The car park at SP 496 132 is halfway down the long, straight road, on your right. If you reach the traffic lights next to the fuel station, you've gone too far.

Oxtail Loop is the kind of ride of which you dream. The route is flat, fast, easy to navigate and littered with postcard views. There are enough dips and climbs to stretch and tighten leg muscles mid-ride, but the quiet country lanes throughout afford effortless riding and constant encouragement to push the pace. The stretch of road from The Fox Inn in Leafield down into Crawley has a high grin-factor, while the narrow road alongside the Windrush River beyond Witney is a hidden gem.

Overview
Easing your way out of Kidlington is easy enough and in no time you're into Cotswold Country with Hampton Poyle, Bletchingdon and Kirtlington being your early markers. After turning left after the River Cherwell in Lower Heyford, the route soon offers up an interesting mix of terrain including a short-sharp climb near Wootton and a cracking time-trial section into Stonesfield. The return leg from Leafield heralds the return of flatter going through to Witney and beyond.

 Exit the leisure centre, turn ➡ along the slip road to a garage and turn ➡ again onto Bicester Road. Turn ⬅ at the T-junction, continue to the roundabout and go ⬆, then take the next ⬅ for **Hampton Poyle** and carry on to **Bletchingdon**. At the junction with the B4027 turn ⬅ then take the second ➡ for Kirtlington and continue to the **A4095**. Turn ➡ through **Kirtlington** then, on exiting the village, turn ⬅ for the Heyfords and continue to a crossroads with the **B4030**.

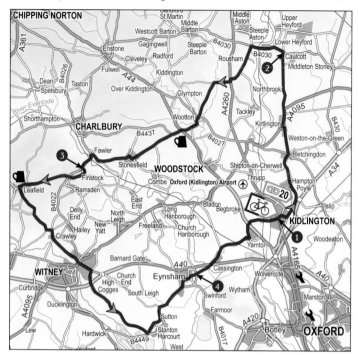

2 Turn ⬅ then ⬅ again into **Lower Heyford** and continue over the long causeway bridge. Turn ⬅ for **Rousham**, continue on to the **A4260** and go ⬆ for Wootton and the crossroads with the **B4027**. Go ⬆. Turn ➡ into

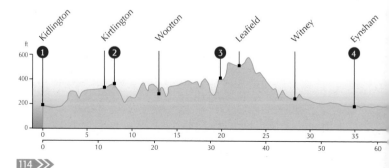

Bletchingdon – continue through the mist and onto Kirtlington

Wootton then ← down to the bridge and continue on up to the **A44**. Go ↑ onto the **B4437** then take the next ← towards Stonesfield. Carry on through **Stonesfield** and then turn ← at the bus stop for Fawler. On exiting **Fawler** turn ← to the **B4022**, turn ← again past Finstock Station and then climb to **Finstock**, turning L into the village.

3 Continue through the village and on up to the B4022 to go ↑ for Leafield. Keep ← at The Fox Inn beside the green in **Leafield** and continue to Crawley. At the memorial in **Crawley** turn → then immediately ← to join the B4022 in **Witney**. Turn → and continue to the crossroads with the **A4095** and go ↑. Continue to the traffic lights and turn → onto Cogges Hill Road for Stanton Harcourt. On reaching **Stanton Harcourt** turn ← onto the **B4449** and continue to the roundabout at **Eynsham**. Turn ← then → at the T-junction and then turn ← onto Mill Street. Turn → onto Newlands Road and continue to the roundabout on the B4449.

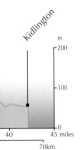

4 Go ↑ along the narrow causeway to the **A40** and go ↑ into **Cassington**. Pass over the railway line into **Yarnton**, turn ← onto Rutten Lane and continue to the roundabout on the A44. Go ↑ to follow Sandy Lane over the Oxford Canal. At the T-junction with the **A4260** in

Witney's hidden gem awaits

The Oxford Canal – a bridge over untroubled waters

Kidlington, turn R and continue to traffic lights. Go ⬆ then filter ⬅ onto the slip road and return to the leisure centre car park.

Link to Route 20

To link to Ox and Bucks simply turn ⬅ onto Bicester Road at the traffic lights beside the garage in **Kidlington** and continue to the roundabout. Turn ➡ at the roundabout and follow the signs for Islip.

Route 20
Ox and Bucks (Oxfordshire and Bucks)

Start/Finish	Kidlington Leisure Centre, Oxford SP 496 132
Distance	111km (69 miles)
Ascent	615m (2020ft)
Grade	
Time	4–5hrs 30mins
Feed stations	The Black Boy, Oving; The Pointer, Brill
Access	From the centre of Oxford, take the A4165 (Banbury Road) north to cross over the A34. At the large roundabout, go SA to follow the road into Kidlington. The car park at SP 496 132 is halfway down the long, straight road, on your right. If you reach the traffic lights next to the fuel station, you've gone too far.

The second route out of Kidlington is a stunning ride that takes full advantage of the flatlands north east of Oxford towards The Vale of Aylesbury. This is cadence training at its best and, with a gentle prevailing south-westerly tailwind, the early miles can be covered with ease. The route of Ox and Bucks is almost entirely ridden on back roads, where the quiet lanes provide good surfaces and easy navigation. The few hills encountered along the way rear up on the return leg, with the two climbs towards Brill being the only earnest challenges.

Overview

Once over the A34 it's a simple case of ticking off the villages as you head north towards Buckingham – Islip, Ambrosden, Marsh Gibbon and Gawcott acting as beacons to guide your way. As you swing right to begin the return journey the navigation is just as kind, with the villages of Oving, Brill, Long Crendon and Oakley showing the way home. But do you remember that tailwind?

1 Turn ➡ out of the car park onto the slip road and turn ➡ onto Bicester Road. Turn ⬅ at a T-junction, continue to a roundabout and turn ➡ over the **A34**, then ➡ again for Islip. At the **B4027** in **Islip** turn ➡ then ⬅ onto Middle Street and continue, going over the **M40** to Ambrosden. Turn ⬅ in **Ambrosden** then immediately ➡ and continue to the **B4011**. Turn ➡ then ⬅ and turn ⬅ again into the village of **Blackthorn**. Continue to the **A41**, turn ➡ then ⬅ under the railway bridge and

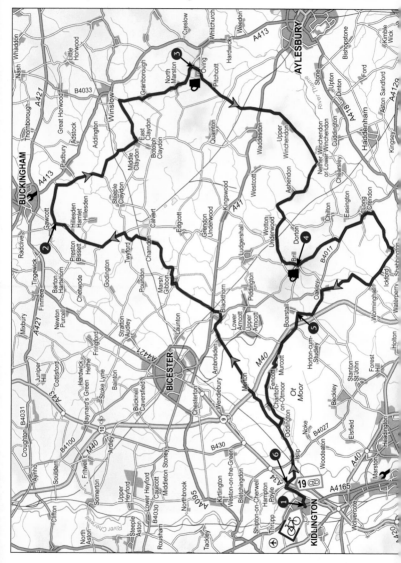

continue to **Marsh Gibbon**. Follow the road ← out of Marsh Gibbon to Charndon. Keep Grebe Lake to your →, go over the railway line, continue to the crossroads and turn ← for Gawcott and Buckingham.

2 At **Gawcott** turn →, signposted Padbury, and turn → again at the ⬑ bend at Laurel Farm, signposted Steeple Claydon and Padbury. Continue to a T-junction and turn →, signposted

Turning right for Ashendon, great descent... and climb!

Steeple Claydon. Continue to a large open crossroads and turn ← onto Sandhill Road, signposted East Claydon. Go over the railway line into **East Claydon** and keep ← through the village towards Winslow. At the T-junction at Tinkers End turn → and continue to **Granborough** and **North Marston** before reaching **Oving**.

3 Turn → in Oving onto Bowling Alley, signposted Pitchcott, continue to a T-junction and turn → to continue to the **A41** near Waddesdon. Go ↑ at the A41 towards Winchendon, continue to the crossroads beyond Upper Winchendon and turn →, signposted Ashendon. At the top of the climb into **Ashendon** turn ← for Dorton and Brill, then descend

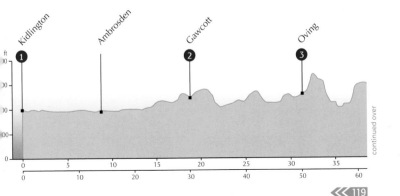

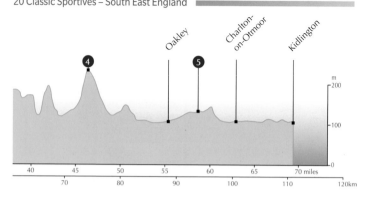

Brick Hill, continuing around the sharp ← bend to a small wood. Turn →, signposted Brill. Continue to follow the signposting for Brill and turn ← up into the village.

4 Keep ← at The Square, descend towards Chilton and Long Crendon to a T-junction with the **B4011** and turn ← for Long Crendon. At The Angel restaurant in **Long Crendon** turn → onto Sandy Lane and descend to **Shabbington**. Turn → at the T-junction, signposted Ickford and Worminghall. At the crossroads in **Worminghall** turn → for Oakley and continue to the T-junction in Oakley. Turn ← onto Oxford Road in **Oakley**, continue to the road junction before the M40 and turn →, signposted Boarstall and Bicester.

5 Continue to a T-junction and turn ←. Cross over the **M40** and then turn immediately → signposted Murcott and MOD Bicester. Continue through **Murcott** to **Charlton-on-Otmoor** and turn ← beside the cemetery. Continue to a crossroads and turn L through **Oddington** and **Islip**. At the **B4027** turn → then ←, retracing your steps onto the Kidlington Road. On reaching the slip road above the **A34**, turn ← and continue to the roundabout.

Link to Route 19

To link to Oxtail Loop turn → at the roundabout, having crossed the **A34** at **Kidlington**, then turn ← to follow signs for Hampton Poyle and Bletchingdon. Turn ← into **Kidlington** and turn → onto Bicester Road. At the traffic lights turn ← to return to the leisure centre car park.

Appendix A
Bike shops and cycle repair outfits

Route 1

Forest Leisure Cycling
Village centre
Burley BH24 4AB
Tel: 01425 403584
hire@forestleisurecycling.co.uk
www.forestleisurecycling.co.uk

Forge Cycleworks
Unit 12D
Furlong Shopping Centre
Ringwood
Hampshire BH24 1AT
Tel: 01425 482797
info@forgecycles.co.uk
www.forgecycles.co.uk

Routes 1–2

Cyclexperience
2 Brookley Road
Brockenhurst
Hampshire SO42 7RR
Tel: 01590 624204/624808
www.cyclex.co.uk

Route 2

AA Bike Hire
FernglenGosport Lane
Lyndhurst
Hampshire SO43 7BL
Tel: 023 8028 3349
www.aabikehirenewforest.co.uk

Figgures Cycles
Henderson Court
Lymington SO41 9FQ
Tel: 01590 672002
www.figgurescycles.co.uk

Route 3

Cycle Surgery
The Boardwalk
Port Solent
Portsmouth
Hampshire PO6 4TP
Tel: 023 9220 5388
portsolent@cyclesurgery.com
www.cyclesurgery.com

Route 4

Bikefixers
Queen Elizabeth Country Park car park
South Downs National Park
Mobile mechanic Sunday mornings only 8am to
12pm (warm weather permitting!)
Tel: 02392 430358
www.bikefixers.co.uk

Route 5

Behind the Bike Shed
22a Marlborough Street
Andover
Hampshire SP10 1DQ
Tel: 01264 338794
enquiries@behindthebikeshed.co.uk
www.behindthebikeshed.co.uk

Routes 6–7

BikeLux
MotorLux Mazda
Ampere Road
London Road Industrial Estate
Newbury
Berkshire RG14 2AE
Tel: 01635 818930
sales@bikelux.co.uk
www.bikelux.co.uk

Newbury Supernova Cycles
4 Oxford Street
Newbury
Berkshire RG14 1JB
Tel: 01635 46600
info@supernovacycles.co.uk
www.supernovacycles.co.uk

Specialized Concept Store
3 & 7 Norman House
Hambridge Road
Newbury RG14 5XA
Tel: 01635 33736
newbury@specializedconceptstore.co.uk
www.specializedconceptstore.co.uk

Route 8
Mountain Mania
10 High Street
Goring
Oxfordshire RG8 9AT
Tel: 01491 871721
www.mountainmaniacycles.co.uk

Routes 8–9
AW Cycles
110 Henley Road
Caversham
Reading
Berkshire RG4 6DH
Tel: 0118 9463050
shop@awcycles.co.uk
www.awcycles.co.uk

Berkshire Bikes
18–20 Wokingham Road
Reading
Berkshire RG45 7AQ
Tel: 0118 9661799
www.berkshirebikes.com

Route 10
Basing Cycles
22 Winchester Street
Basingstoke
Hampshire RG21 7DY
Tel: 01256 465266
www.basingcycles.co.uk

Liphook Cycles
16 The Square
Liphook
Hampshire GU30 7AHT
el: 01428 727858
www.liphookcycles.com

Pedal Heaven
311–313 Fleet Road
Fleet GU51 3BU
Tel: 012526 285575
shop@pedalheaven.co.uk
www.pedalheaven.co.uk

Route 11
Cycle Works
19–21 West Street
Haslemere GU27 2AB
Tel: 01428 648424
www.cycleworks.co.uk

Halfords
2–6 High Street
Godalming
Surrey GU7 1ED
Tel: 01483 415752
www.halfords.com

Route 12
Evans Cycles
50–52 The Broadway
Crawley
West Sussex RH10 1HD
Tel: 01293 574900
contactcentreteam@evanscycles.com
www.evanscycles.com

Head for the Hills
43–44 West Street
Dorking
Surrey RH4 1BU
Tel: 01306 885007
shop@head-for-the-hills.co.uk
www.head-for-the-hills.co.uk

Route 13
C&N Cycles
32 Station Road
Redhill
Surrey RH1 1PD
Tel: 01737 760857
www.candncycles.co.uk

Route 14
Haywards Heath Cycle Centre
34–36 The Broadway
Haywards Heath
West Sussex RH16 3AL
Tel: 01444 457777
info@haywardsheathcyclecentre.com
www.haywardsheathcyclecentre.com

South Coast Bikes
2 Quayside Buildings
Basin Road South
Hove
Brighton
East Sussex BN41 1WF
Tel: 01273 202124
enquiries@southcoastbikes.co.uk
www.southcoastbikes.co.uk

Sydney Street Bikes
24 Sydney Street
Hove
Brighton
East Sussex BN1 4EN
Tel: 01273 624700
infohove@sydneystreetbikes.co.uk
www.sydneystreetbikes.co.uk

Route 15

The Bike Warehouse
53 High Street
Sevenoaks
Kent TN13 1JF
Tel: 01732 464997
www.thebikewarehouse.net

DNA Cycles
91a High Street
Maidstone
Kent SL6 1JX
Tel: 01628 780026
mail@dnacycles.co.uk
www.dnacycles.co.uk

Wildside Cycles
77–83 Camden Road
Royal Tunbridge Wells
Kent TN1 2QL
Tel: 01892 527069
sales@wildside-online.co.uk
www.wildside-online.co.uk

Route 16

Evolution Cycles
23a Cavendish Place
Eastbourne
East Sussex BN21 3EJ
Tel: 01323 737320
info@evocycles.co.uk
www.evocycles.co.uk

Kontour Cycles
74 High Street
Polegate
East Sussex BN26 6AA
Tel: 01323 482368
info@kontourcycles.co.uk
www.kontourcycles.co.uk

Route 17

Stows Cycles
209 Dedworth Road
Windsor
Berkshire SL4 4JW

Tel: 01753 862734
stowswindsor@tiscali.co.uk
www.stows.co.uk

Routes 17–18

Saddle Safari
9 Dean Street
Marlow
Buckinghamshire SL7 3AA
Tel: 01628 533003
info@saddlesafari.co.uk
www.saddlesafari.co.uk

Route 18

Buckingham Bikes
3&4 Villiers Buildings
Buckingham Street
Aylesbury
Buckinghamshire HP20 2LE
Tel: 01296 482077
info@buckinghambikes.com
www.buckinghambikes.com

The Bicycle Workshop (Cycle Fleet)
Rookwood
Frith Hill
Great Missenden
Buckinghamshire HP16 9AW
Tel: 01494 868607
www.cyclefleet.com

Routes 19–20

Beeline Bikes
205 Cowley Road
Oxford
Oxfordshire OX4 1XA
Tel: 01865 246615
www.beelinebicycles.co.uk
Summertown Cycles

00–202 Banbury Road
Oxford
Oxfordshire OX2 7BY
Tel: 01865 316885
www.summertowncycles.co.uk

Route 20

VeloTEC Mobile Cycling Service
12 Swan Close
Buckingham
Buckinghamshire MK18 7EP
Tel: 07525 437579
info@velotec-uk.com
www.velotec-uk.com

Appendix B
Useful contacts

Sportive cycling websites

British Cycling

www.britishcycling.org.uk, the website of Britain's cycling governing body, is a real mine of sportive information. You'll find a comprehensive events calendar, plus a whole load of training and nutrition tips. The website is simple to navigate, easy to read and features clear instructions on how to enter.

Cyclosport

The Cyclosport website – www.cyclosport.org – has an excellent 'magazine' look to it. It's not only full of features on sportive events at home and abroad, but also bikes and kit. A really useful website aimed at those riders with a little more experience, due to the continental European element, but an excellent and informative website for the sportive rider nonetheless.

UKcyclingevents

UKcyclingevents (www.ukcyclingevents.co.uk) is the home of one of the UK's premier sportive event organisers. The website is heavy on sponsorship, but at least you know what you're getting for your money when you sign on and collect your goodie bag.

road.cc

www.road.cc is full of the latest news from road cycling and sportives. With plenty of reviews to get a head on what's worth buying there's always something worth reading. The website, fresh and very appealing, is fun and informative to read whether you're a weekend warrior or a cannibal on the bike.

Cycling Weekly

One of the UK's most popular magazines, *Cycling Weekly* also has a life of its own on the internet, at www.cyclingweekly.co.uk. This website is packed with features on bikes, clothing, kit, components, you name it; great articles on nutrition too. A full events calendar complements the information overload. It is a real one-stop shop for sportive riders.

Tourist information

For a list of all the tourist information centres in the region as well as details of events, things to do, accommodation options and even great pubs, go to www.visitsoutheastengland.com.

Accommodation websites

www.visitsoutheastengland.com/accommodation

www.thenewforest.co.uk/accommodation

www.visit-hampshire.co.uk/where-to-stay

www.westsussex.info/hotels/
    bed-and-breakfast.shtml

www.visitoxfordandoxfordshire.com/
    accommodation

www.visitkent.co.uk/places-to-stay

www.visitsurrey.com/accommodation

Hospitals with A&E facilities

East Surrey Hospital
Canada Avenue
Redhill
Surrey RH1 5RH
Tel: 01737 768511

John Radcliffe Hospital
Headley Way
Headington
Oxford OX3 9DU
Tel: 01865 741166

Maidstone Hospital
Hermitage Lane
Maidstone
Kent ME16 9QQ
Tel: 01622 729000

Royal Berkshire Hospital
London Road
Reading RG1 5AN
Tel: 0118 322 5111

Southampton General Hospital
Tremona Road
Southampton
Hampshire SO16 6YD
Tel: 023 8077 7222

BRITISH ISLES CHALLENGES, COLLECTIONS AND ACTIVITIES

The End to End Trail
The Mountains of England and Wales: 1&2
The National Trails
The Relative Hills of Britain
The Ridges of England, Wales and Ireland
The UK Trailwalker's Handbook
The UK's County Tops
Three Peaks, Ten Tors

UK CYCLING

20 Classic Sportive Rides
  South West England
  South East England
Border Country Cycle Routes
Cycling in the Cotswolds
Cycling in the Hebrides
Cycling in the Peak District
Cycling in the Yorkshire Dales
Cycling the Pennine Bridleway
Mountain Biking in the Lake District
Mountain Biking in the Yorkshire Dales
Mountain Biking on the North Downs
Mountain Biking on the South Downs
The C2C Cycle Route
The End to End Cycle Route
The Lancashire Cycleway

SCOTLAND

Backpacker's Britain
  Central and Southern Scottish Highlands
  Northern Scotland
Ben Nevis and Glen Coe
Great Mountain Days in Scotland
Not the West Highland Way
Scotland's Best Small Mountains
Scotland's Far West
Scotland's Mountain Ridges
Scrambles in Lochaber
The Ayrshire and Arran Coastal Paths
The Border Country
The Cape Wrath Trail
The Great Glen Way
The Isle of Mull
The Isle of Skye
The Pentland Hills
The Skye Trail

The Southern Upland Way
The Speyside Way
The West Highland Way
Walking Highland Perthshire
Walking in Scotland's Far North
Walking in the Angus Glens
Walking in the Cairngorms
Walking in the Ochils, Campsie Fells and Lomond Hills
Walking in the Southern Uplands
Walking in Torridon
Walking Loch Lomond and the Trossachs
Walking on Harris and Lewis
Walking on Jura, Islay and Colonsay
Walking on Rum and the Small Isles
Walking on the Isle of Arran
Walking on the Orkney and Shetland Isles
Walking on Uist and Barra
Walking the Corbetts
  1 South of the Great Glen
  2 North of the Great Glen
Walking the Galloway Hills
Walking the Lowther Hills
Walking the Munros
  1 Southern, Central and Western Highlands
  2 Northern Highlands and the Cairngorms
Winter Climbs Ben Nevis and Glen Coe
Winter Climbs in the Cairngorms
World Mountain Ranges: Scotland

NORTHERN ENGLAND TRAILS

A Northern Coast to Coast Walk
Hadrian's Wall Path
The Dales Way
The Pennine Way

NORTH EAST ENGLAND, YORKSHIRE DALES AND PENNINES

Great Mountain Days in the Pennines
Historic Walks in North Yorkshire
South Pennine Walks
St Oswald's Way and St Cuthbert's Way
The Cleveland Way and the Yorkshire Wolds Way
The North York Moors
The Reivers Way
The Teesdale Way

The Yorkshire Dales
  North and East
  South and West
Walking in County Durham
Walking in Northumberland
Walking in the North Pennines
Walks in Dales Country
Walks in the Yorkshire Dales
Walks on the North York Moors – Books 1 & 2

NORTH WEST ENGLAND AND THE ISLE OF MAN

Historic Walks in Cheshire
Isle of Man Coastal Path
The Isle of Man
The Lune Valley and Howgills
The Ribble Way
Walking in Cumbria's Eden Valley
Walking in Lancashire
Walking in the Forest of Bowland and Pendle
Walking on the West Pennine Moors
Walks in Lancashire Witch Country
Walks in Ribble Country
Walks in Silverdale and Arnside
Walks in the Forest of Bowland

LAKE DISTRICT

Coniston Copper Mines
Great Mountain Days in the Lake District
Lake District: High Fell Walks
Lake District: Low Level and Lake Walks
Lake District Winter Climbs
Lakeland Fellranger
  The Central Fells
  The Far-Eastern Fells
  The Mid-Western Fells
  The Near Eastern Fells
  The Northern Fells
  The North-Western Fells
  The Southern Fells
  The Western Fells

Roads and Tracks of the
    Lake District
Rocky Rambler's Wild Walks
Scrambles in the Lake District
    North & South
Short Walks in Lakeland
    1 South Lakeland
    2 North Lakeland
    3 West Lakeland
The Cumbria Coastal Way
The Cumbria Way
Tour of the Lake District

DERBYSHIRE, PEAK DISTRICT AND MIDLANDS

High Peak Walks
Scrambles in the Dark Peak
The Star Family Walks
Walking in Derbyshire
White Peak Walks
    The Northern Dales
    The Southern Dales

SOUTHERN ENGLAND

Suffolk Coast & Heaths Walks
The Cotswold Way
The Great Stones Way
The North Downs Way
The Peddars Way and Norfolk
    Coast Path
The Ridgeway National Trail
The South Downs Way
The South West Coast Path
The Thames Path
The Two Moors Way
Walking in Essex
Walking in Kent
Walking in Norfolk
Walking in Sussex
Walking in the Chilterns
Walking in the Cotswolds
Walking in the Isles of Scilly
Walking in the New Forest
Walking in the Thames Valley
Walking on Dartmoor
Walking on Guernsey
Walking on Jersey
Walking on the Isle of Wight
Walks in the South Downs
    National Park

WALES AND WELSH BORDERS

Glyndwr's Way
Great Mountain Days
    in Snowdonia
Hillwalking in Snowdonia

Hillwalking in Wales: 1&2
Offa's Dyke Path
Ridges of Snowdonia
Scrambles in Snowdonia
The Ascent of Snowdon
The Ceredigion and Snowdonia
    Coast Paths
Lleyn Peninsula Coastal Path
Pembrokeshire Coastal Path
The Severn Way
The Shropshire Hills
The Wye Valley Walk
Walking in Pembrokeshire
Walking in the Forest of Dean
Walking in the South Wales
    Valleys
Walking in the Wye Valley
Walking on Gower
Walking on the Brecon Beacons
Welsh Winter Climbs

INTERNATIONAL CHALLENGES, COLLECTIONS AND ACTIVITIES

Canyoning
Canyoning in the Alps
Europe's High Points
The Via Francigena: 1&2

EUROPEAN CYCLING

Cycle Touring in France
Cycle Touring in Ireland
Cycle Touring in Spain
Cycle Touring in Switzerland
Cycling in the French Alps
Cycling the Canal du Midi
Cycling the River Loire
The Danube Cycleway Vol 1
The Grand Traverse of the
    Massif Central
The Moselle Cycle Route
The Rhine Cycle Route
The Way of St James

AFRICA

Climbing in the Moroccan Anti-
    Atlas
Kilimanjaro
Mountaineering in the Moroccan
    High Atlas
The High Atlas
Trekking in the Atlas Mountains
Walking in the Drakensberg

ALPS – CROSS-BORDER ROUTES

100 Hut Walks in the Alps
Across the Eastern Alps: E5

Alpine Points of View
Alpine Ski Mountaineering
    1 Western Alps
    2 Central and Eastern Alps
Chamonix to Zermatt
Snowshoeing
Tour of Mont Blanc
Tour of the Matterhorn
Trekking in the Alps
Trekking in the Silvretta and
    Rätikon Alps
Walking in the Alps
Walks and Treks in the
    Maritime Alps

PYRENEES AND FRANCE/SPAIN CROSS-BORDER ROUTES

Rock Climbs in the Pyrenees
The GR10 Trail
The GR11 Trail – La Senda
The Mountains of Andorra
The Pyrenean Haute Route
The Pyrenees
The Way of St James:
    France & Spain
Walks and Climbs in the Pyrenees

AUSTRIA

The Adlerweg
Trekking in Austria's Hohe Tauern
Trekking in the Stubai Alps
Trekking in the Zillertal Alps
Walking in Austria

BELGIUM AND LUXEMBOURG

Walking in the Ardennes

EASTERN EUROPE

The High Tatras
The Mountains of Romania
Walking in Bulgaria's
    National Parks
Walking in Hungary

FRANCE

Chamonix Mountain Adventures
Ecrins National Park
Mont Blanc Walks
Mountain Adventures in
    the Maurienne
The Cathar Way
The GR20 Corsica
The GR5 Trail
The Robert Louis Stevenson Trail
Tour of the Oisans: The GR54
Tour of the Queyras
Tour of the Vanoise

Trekking in the Vosges and Jura
Vanoise Ski Touring
Via Ferratas of the French Alps
Walking in Corsica
Walking in Provence – East
Walking in Provence – West
Walking in the Auvergne
Walking in the Cevennes
Walking in the Dordogne
Walking in the Haute Savoie –
    North & South
Walking in the Languedoc
Walking in the Tarentaise and
    Beaufortain Alps
Walks in the Cathar Region

GERMANY
Germany's Romantic Road
Hiking and Biking in the
    Black Forest
Walking in the Bavarian Alps

HIMALAYA
Annapurna
Bhutan
Everest
Garhwal and Kumaon
Langtang with Gosainkund
    and Helambu
Manaslu
The Mount Kailash Trek
Trekking in Ladakh
Trekking in the Himalaya

ICELAND & GREENLAND
Trekking in Greenland
Walking and Trekking in Iceland

IRELAND
Irish Coastal Walks
The Irish Coast to Coast Walk
The Mountains of Ireland

ITALY
Gran Paradiso
Sibillini National Park
Shorter Walks in the Dolomites
Through the Italian Alps
Trekking in the Apennines
Trekking in the Dolomites
Via Ferratas of the Italian
    Dolomites: Vols 1 & 2
Walking in Abruzzo
Walking in Italy's Stelvio
    National Park
Walking in Sardinia
Walking in Sicily

Walking in the Central
    Italian Alps
Walking in the Dolomites
Walking in Tuscany
Walking in Umbria
Walking on the Amalfi Coast
Walking the Italian Lakes

MEDITERRANEAN
Jordan – Walks, Treks, Caves,
    Climbs and Canyons
The Ala Dag
The High Mountains of Crete
The Mountains of Greece
Treks and Climbs in Wadi Rum
Walking in Malta
Western Crete

NORTH AMERICA
British Columbia
The Grand Canyon
The John Muir Trail
The Pacific Crest Trail

SOUTH AMERICA
Aconcagua and the
    Southern Andes
Hiking and Biking Peru's
    Inca Trails
Torres del Paine

SCANDINAVIA
Walking in Norway
Slovenia, Croatia and Montenegro
The Islands of Croatia
The Julian Alps of Slovenia
The Mountains of Montenegro
Trekking in Slovenia
Walking in Croatia
Walking in Slovenia: The
    Karavanke

SPAIN AND PORTUGAL
Costa Blanca: West
Mountain Walking in
    Southern Catalunya
The Mountains of Central Spain
The Mountains of Nerja
The Northern Caminos
Trekking through Mallorca
Walking in Madeira
Walking in Mallorca
Walking in Menorca
Walking in the Algarve
Walking in the Cordillera
    Cantabrica
Walking in the Sierra Nevada

Walking on Gran Canaria
Walking on La Gomera and
    El Hierro
Walking on La Palma
Walking on Lanzarote and
    Fuerteventura
Walking on Tenerife
Walking the GR7 in Andalucia
Walks and Climbs in the
    Picos de Europa

SWITZERLAND
Alpine Pass Route
Central Switzerland
The Bernese Alps
The Swiss Alps
Tour of the Jungfrau Region
Walking in the Valais
Walking in Ticino
Walks in the Engadine

TECHNIQUES
Geocaching in the UK
Indoor Climbing
Lightweight Camping
Map and Compass
Mountain Weather
Moveable Feasts
Outdoor Photography
Polar Exploration
Rock Climbing
Sport Climbing
The Book of the Bivvy
The Hillwalker's Guide to
    Mountaineering
The Hillwalker's Manual

MINI GUIDES
Alpine Flowers
Avalanche!
Navigating with a GPS
Navigation
Pocket First Aid and
    Wilderness Medicine
Snow

MOUNTAIN LITERATURE
8000 metres
A Walk in the Clouds
Unjustifiable Risk?

For full information on all our
guides, books and eBooks,
visit our website:
www.cicerone.co.uk.

Walking – Trekking – Mountaineering – Climbing – Cycling

Over 40 years, Cicerone have built up an outstanding collection of 300 guides, inspiring all sorts of amazing adventures.

Every guide comes from extensive exploration and research by our expert authors, all with a passion for their subjects. They are frequently praised, endorsed and used by clubs, instructors and outdoor organisations.

All our titles can now be bought as **e-books** and many as iPad and Kindle files and we will continue to make all our guides available for these and many other devices.

Our website shows any **new information** we've received since a book was published. Please do let us know if you find anything has changed, so that we can pass on the latest details. On our **website** you'll also find some great ideas and lots of information, including sample chapters, contents lists, reviews, articles and a photo gallery.

It's easy to keep in touch with what's going on at Cicerone, by getting our monthly **free e-newsletter**, which is full of offers, competitions, up-to-date information and topical articles. You can subscribe on our home page and also follow us on **Facebook** and **Twitter**, as well as our **blog**.

Cicerone – the very best guides for exploring the world.

CICERONE

2 Police Square Milnthorpe Cumbria LA7 7PY
Tel: 015395 62069 info@cicerone.co.uk
www.cicerone.co.uk